A Heart
Worth Entering
Heaven

Not Perfect but Faithful

A. CUMMINGS

WESTBOW
PRESS®
A DIVISION OF THOMAS NELSON
& ZONDERVAN

WestBow Press books may be ordered through booksellers or by contacting:

WestBow Press
A Division of Thomas Nelson & Zondervan
1663 Liberty Drive
Bloomington, IN 47403
www.westbowpress.com
1 (866) 928-1240

ISBN: 978-1-9736-5760-6 (sc)
ISBN: 978-1-9736-5770-5 (hc)
ISBN: 978-1-9736-5761-3 (e)

Library of Congress Control Number: 2019903388

Print information available on the last page.

WestBow Press rev. date: 4/24/2019

This book is dedicated to the men and women who
are striving to be a part of the remnant.

Offer the sacrifices of righteousness
and put your trust in the Lord.
(Psm 4:5)

God bless us all

Contents

Chapter 1   Making Sense of It All 1

Chapter 2   Heartthrob 13

Chapter 3   Lovesick 21

Chapter 4   Holiness! 31

Chapter 5   Happy Days 41

Chapter 6   Power of the Pen 45

Chapter 7   Called! 51

Chapter 8   I Care 59

Chapter 9   Anger 67

Chapter 10   Divorce Papers 77

Chapter 11   Baggage 83

Chapter 12   The First 24 Hours 97

Chapter 13   Only Jesus 103

Chapter 14   Reasonable Action 111

Chapter 15   Marriage 115

Introduction

Before you read this book, please do me the kind favor of praying first. Pray while reading it, pray when you put it down, and pray when you pick it back up. Pray when you finish reading it and I pray that you will read it again. In all sincerity, beseech God to perform in you what this book is intended to do: To allow the ministry of the Holy Spirit to quicken in your soul the realization of God's deep desire for you to live a life that honors Him in all you do, especially in relationships and above all in marriage.

You will undoubtedly be entertained, but do not lose sight of the real purpose of this book, which is to change the way you look at marriage, infidelity, and divorce. It is my prayer that you will be inspired to diligently seek a loving and faithful relationship with God that will abundantly spill over into your marriage.

Stay alert:

- You will want to see God as He reveals Himself in this story.
- Be open to what God is speaking to your heart.
- Look at and evaluate your marriage (relationship) through God's eyes.

I must warn you, if you do not come prayed up, with an open heart, open mind, and keeping it real (with yourself), you will not take away the riches that God has for you. God chose this forum to speak to you in the privacy of your own space, so be honest with yourself and with God as you read. Remember, this is a private conversation with you and God, via my story.

Once we understand that marriage is not ours, but rather given to us as a scared gift, we will then begin to treat it with the honor it deserves. God did not create marriage to fit into your life, but your life is to fit into the context of the marriage vows. The vows are "till death do us part," God is able to sustain your marriage to its natural conclusion.

Marriage was created to be good and is meant to honor and glorify God. There is no honor in infidelity and divorce. There is no honor when we debase, devalue, cause injury, pain, and chaos in what was supposed to be a bit of paradise on earth.

Failed marriages hurt so many people. A father gives in holy matrimony his daughter to her groom with the expectation that he will be as good to her as he is to himself. *"For no man ever yet hated his own flesh, but nourish and cherish it"* (Eph 5:29). Mothers have a special relationship with their sons, she does not want a woman mistreating her baby! They hesitantly, entrust their son's into the hands of a woman who they hope will be his biggest supporter and encourager. *"Wives, submit yourselves to your own husbands as you do to the Lord. For the husband is the head..."* Eph 5:22). There can only be one head, two heads on one body is not a pretty sight.

We love the idea of marriage, but we do not reverence the institute of marriage. We have failed miserably at protecting the sanctity of marriage. We want marriage on our own terms not on God's or anyone else's. Even though we live in a nation of entitlement and privilege, marriage can never be a one-way street. Yet, when we cannot have it our way, we feel justified in walking away.

Walking away from a marriage is not a crime. Breaking someone's heart is not a crime, tearing a home apart is not a crime, leaving your children is not a crime, and adultery is not a crime. Yet, I tell you the truth, it is a crime, not only before God, but also against God.

Now, shall we get down to what most of you really want to talk about? Does God sanction remarriages - especially if it came about as a direct result of the demise of a marriage? The answer is yes; however, something is required.

My dear one, God is giving you this book because He loves you and desires that you start today on your journey to restoration in your soul and unhindered pleasure in your current marriage. God desires that you live whole in His forgiveness and experience His wonderful blessings upon your life, and in your marriage.

With God's help and through this story I can lay out before you the path to restoration and peace. With God's help, my story will empower you and strengthen you to look at your own life story from God's perspective only, not yours, not your spouse's, and not your best friend's.

I am excited for you! What a great adventure that lies ahead for you and your spouse as you rediscover your marriage, God's way! Start enjoying the relationship that God desires you to have with Him – one of truth and freedom, and no condemnation.

Foreword

J. Alfred Smith, Sr., Pastor Emeritus
Allen Temple Baptist Church
Oakland, CA

Ms. Cummings is an excellent writer with a very helpful message. She is transparent in sharing the highs and the lows of her life. She is careful to describe those events of her life that she deeply regrets. But, she lifts our spirits in detailing how she learned from those negative experiences what to do to rise high above the failures of the past.

Because she had the courage to share, readers will receive unexpected riches. You will see the loving kindness, mercy, and protection of God in the events of her life. You will not miss how Ms. Cummings' walk with God enriched her life with spiritual discipline, intimacy, and obedience. You will understand how faith works and how true faith is more than church membership. Reading this book will make you wiser in combating the pitfalls and satanic deceptions of the world, and to be truly victorious in overcoming gravitational forces seeking to pull you down. You will discover the secret for living the abundant life. You will thank Ms. Cummings for sharing her moving and beautiful story.

CHAPTER I

Making Sense of It All

It was late one night, about two weeks before Del left home, when I finally gave in to the pain. I had plenty of sleepless nights in the last few years, but this night was different. There would be no rest and no sleep, the showdown (or should I say meltdown) had come. Tonight I was going to make some sense out of what was happening to my life. My marriage was falling apart right in front of me; it was like trying to pick up jell-o with your fingers, the more you handle it the quicker it dissolves. Del had made up his mind to leave home and there was nothing more I could do or say to change that.

Anyway, how could I change anything when I did not know what the problem was? At this point whether I knew or not no longer mattered, Del was determined to follow through with his plans. It made me ill to think about it, but it was time to admit that my marriage was beyond human repair. The confession punched a hole in the place holding what I was not ready to deal with. Gushing out and spilling over the pain came; consequently, this would be a night unlike no other.

My mind was like a traffic jam, questions were backed-up as far as one could see. I had no answers, only questions that led to more questions: What did I do? Can we work it out? What will people think? What will I do without him? How could this be happening to me? I was weary of all the questions, for months the questions plagued me, one after the other, on this night they all joined forces and demanded answers. My mind was screaming back, "Go away, and leave me alone. I don't have any *answers for you!"* I was sick from fretting, riddled with anxiety and worn out from years of trying to keep it all together. My future was hanging in the balance dependent on the actions of another human being, who by the way was lying next to me sound asleep.

I had to go to work the next morning and needed to get some sleep, but my emotions had kicked into overdrive. The pain was unleashed and in full control. My world was upside down and I needed to know why. The man who once adored me would not talk to me, let alone acknowledge my suffering. Satan was destroying our marriage and Del was asleep!

I wanted to grab hold of his shoulders and shake him to bring him to his senses, and yes, I wanted to plead with him one more time, *"Don't let satan destroy us. Help me fight for our marriage. Del, wake up!"* Although I had completely given in to the pain, I knew if Del woke up to such a pitiful scene, he would have viewed it as a grand performance. The pain was too raw to risk having it disparaged. I dared not awaken him, which infuriated me and exacerbated the anguish I was already in the grips of.

No way was this the same man I had eagerly vowed to spend the rest of my life with. This was no childhood fantasy, forty-two years later I felt the same about Del as I did the first time I laid eyes on him. He was my husband, but he was also my hero. The hero who used to show up in my dreams was now my tormentor.

Thoughts of how we met along with memories of better times were strangling me. I was overwhelmed with grief and bitter disappointment. My emotions could no longer remain pent up. I burst wide open and could not turn back even if I wanted to. In reality, I needed to let it out, burdens can only be carried for so long, eventually something has to give. I was a mess, my pillow was soaked with tears and snot, and my heart was suffocating in the disappointment of being let down by the man I trusted.

While sobbing uncontrollably through clenched teeth an unfamiliar voice from within begin to plead with God, *"Lord, please tell me what I did to this man? I have been a faithful wife. I loved Del when he became un-loveable. I have been kind to him when he was not very nice to me. I put up with him when I should have been the one leaving!"* I laid myself open to help Del understand me and bent over backwards to get along with

2

him, only to have him leave. I could not wrap my brain around what was happening to my life.

Lying there in dejection I begin to think about how Jacob must have felt on that night he wrestled with the angel of God until daybreak (Gen 32:24-26). I was prepared to duke it out all night too. Like Jacob, I was as desperate and afraid as he must have been. Jacob was not going to face Esau without first hearing from God; I was not willing to face another day without hearing from Him.

Like falling into a black hole, I could feel myself sinking further into despair. I did not want to hear what anyone else had to say. I was becoming weary of others' take on Del's behavior, only God knew what the problem was. At this point, I did not even want to hear what Del had to say! If he finally had something to say, this was the wrong time to say it. I was hurting and now I was mad. I trusted this man with my life! I was out done with him and even more so with myself. My weakness and neediness sickened me. My life is not ending just because Del is leaving. If he wants to go, let him go! To no avail, I tried to check myself, "Why do you want someone who clearly doesn't want you? What is wrong with you? Girl, have some pride!"

When it was time to fight for our marriage Del left. It was as though our life together never existed. I was trying hard to make sense out of what was senseless. Yet, it really boiled down to one question. Del leaving and not wanting the marriage was painful, but that was not the root of the torment. Among the many questions backed up in my head, the burning one that took me to the edge was still on the table. Del never told me unequivocally what his issue was with me. My marriage was ending and I did not know why. I was a faceless character whose role had ended. Without an explanation, I was written out of the script and my contract was null.

Nothing good between us, nothing precious about our marriage warranted a reason for its demise. I had to endure insult to injury and to me that was unconscionable. No one can say what he or she does not deserve, but I will say it anyway, "I did not deserve this."

I know God can change any situation. The Bible says when in the Lord's hand, the king's heart can turn in any direction God desires (Prov 21:1). I prayed many nights for God to turn Del's heart back to me. God is for marriage, it is His institute and I was certain He would eventually turn our marriage around. *"This is a test, God is working on Del,"* I would tell myself. It was Del God had the issue with not me. I had convinced myself that I was in the crossfire of God's work on Del, so I had to be patient and ride it out. I could not have been more wrong. Disobedient me, it was as much about me as it was about Del. I made it about me when I stepped in the middle of something I knew nothing about.

My mind was leaping from one scenario to the next. It was late and I was exhausted, but I could not stay in bed another second. There was no rest, least of all in bed and most of all not lying there next to Del. I was trapped, nowhere to turn, too late to turn back and no reason to go forward.

My breathing was becoming difficult; was I actually starting to hyperventilate! This is too much drama! Then I realized I needed to get my face out of my pillow. Although burying my face muffled the sounds of crying it had not occurred to me it might also cut off my air supply. Talk about out of touch. I had to get on my feet to clear my head, yet I could not get out of bed.

It was getting later in the night and it did not appear as if I was going to get any answers. The thought of not hearing from God was unbearable and upset me that much more. I abhorred the thought of another day coming and I was no closer to knowing why Del was behaving so badly toward me. I was restless and needed to get up from what felt like a bed of nails. *"Why can't I get up? Oh, great, now I have to deal with my body not cooperating. It's bad enough my mind is racing out of control. My pillow is soaked, I have a runny nose that needs wiping, and now my legs feel like they are stuck in cement."*

After several attempts to get up, I realized I did not have the strength to get myself out of bed. I had come to the end of myself and so exhausted I could not muster up enough energy to get up. I was stuck in the middle of the floor on one side and Del asleep on the other side. *"Lord, this is so unfair, when I finally dig my heels in determined to get answers, this is what I get, really?"*

I lost track of time, all I know is it was a long night. I honestly cannot tell you when He came and I do not know how long I laid there unable to move. At some point stillness settled around me, calmness replaced anxiety and I could breathe freely again. The tears stopped flowing and the runny nose dried up. I was lying there in the dark on my back, eyes wide open trying to pierce the darkness then He spoke. With nothing left in me, God could now pour in. **WISDOM CRIES OUT:** *God is the most skillful of surgeons. He knows just where to cut us, what instruments to use for the incision, how deep to cut, while all along the way controlling the bleeding and the heart rate. He knows how much blood, sweat, and tears we can lose and how much pressure our hearts can take. When we want to die because life is too painful, the Surgeon knows you shall live and not die. (Expounded from Job 5:17-18)*

I can say without a doubt, God took me to the brink that night, but the skilled Surgeon would not lose me. Instead He was starting in earnestness the process of restoration (repentance had already come). He knew what I did not; I could take everything He was allowing me to go through even the breaking of my heart. For truly, this would be the night God allowed my heart to be broken, it was for my sake and would be for His glory.

What prompted me to write this particular book was God's answer to my question, *"What did I do?"* Before I share His response, let me first say this, *"We must stop giving all our attention to our pain."* We get entangled in *our* disappointment and *our* pain when life does not go as *we* planned, and we fail to see God's hand in it. We fail to see that He has a purpose for us far greater than the one we so desperately want to cling too. We fail to flow, while in our pain, in the direction God is trying to move us. Nevertheless, He does not give up on us, but uses us still, and in much pain, we birth His purpose. For those of us who decide to develop a real walk with God, be on notice, He takes that commitment seriously and is ready to do His part (usually before you are ready to yours).

You see the real reason Del was leaving had to come from God not from Del or anyone else. Had it come from man, no matter how distasteful or devastating the reason, it would have been on a human level and accepted as such. *"He found someone else,"* or *"he's just going through what men his age go through,"* or *"people grow apart,"* the courts just call it *irreconcilable differences.* To the world, although it does not ease the pain or repair the damage broken marriages cause, these excuses are acceptable norms.

Does anyone seek the spiritual reasons for failed marriages? We have to fight satan on the spiritual battlefield, or in this earthly life, we will lose every time. Satan wants marriages more than anything else we have including our money and our children because when he gets the marriage he gets it all. God honored man and woman with marriage and it is our responsibility to glorify God in that marriage. Divorce, as well as ungodly marriages compromises the holy institute that God designed marriage to be.

God wants to lift our hearts and minds heavenward and re-establish integrity and holiness in marriages. God did not want, and in this case, would not allow human reasons to overshadow, diminish, or worse, dismiss the spiritual reasons for my broken marriage (and countless others). If we miss God's answer, to our discredit we will remain justified in treating the institute of marriage indifferent at best and with contempt at worse.

Sometimes in order for us to come up in our spiritual thinking, the Surgeon has to bring us down. Consequently, God used two people beginning the summer of '71 to this very point, to tell the world we have brought scandal upon what was supposed to be sacred. We have tampered with what was to be tamper-proof. We have manipulated for our own agendas what was to be uncompromising.

Yes, God answered, He spoke straight to my heart. *"You offended me by inviting a married man into your bed. I have plans for you and what you did does not negate those plans. You are being held accountable for your indiscretion and purified of your offense while fulfilling those plans."* Get this, not after fulfilling those plans, not before fulfilling those plans, but simultaneously! Really! Yet, conviction struck the cords of my soul. The compulsion to write this book fell on me like a crushing weight, which was lifted only when writing.

I clearly understood what God was saying, and it struck me instantly, the restoration process can be by fire, was I in the fire, you bet I was. There was only one thing to do, I yielded and simply said, *"Let the will of the Lord be done."* It was time to stop running from the truth. God had what He wanted from me 20 years earlier, my attention! **WISDOM CRIES OUT:** *Twenty years is a big chunk of time out of our lives to be going in the wrong direction.*

The first day Del came into my home I sincerely thought once married God would bless my husband and me. My dear readers, I know you have heard it before; however, sometimes hearing something from a different source is when it hits home. *God is holy and He will not bless your mess.* Yet! He is faithful to forgive and even cleanup your mess. However, and I know I have some witnesses, the cleanup is never how you expected it to be and it never feels good.

Abraham is a witness! Ask him if it felt good when he had to send Ishmael away. God will clean up your mess, but He will not always remove it from your life. Sometimes our mess, though cleaned up, is ever before us as a reminder of our lack of trust in God. The descendants of Abraham to this day are dealing with the descendants of Ishmael.

Although God has cleaned up some of your messes, they are forever before you; a whole lot of folks paying child support for children who do not live in their household. All the step-families, blended families, half siblings, and Lord, the baby momma drama! Some folks have been married three and four times and have children from all marriages. There are countless children from outside marriages, whose parents have moved on to other relationships (having more children). The scenarios are too numerous to list. It is so stressful when children from these relationships have life events that warrant the gathering of *all* family members. Graduations, birthdays, weddings can turn into family feuds. Planning a wedding is a headache! The groom does not want to offend anyone, he loves both sides of the family, but is it safe to invite all sides to the wedding for fear a fight will break out! A daughter is torn between who will walk her down the aisle, her biological father, her former stepfather or the current man in her mother's life! It is a mess, this stuff is from the pit of where satan resides, and certainly does not honor God.

Be aware of how God moves in your life, and as the pieces of your life come together, you will certainly see Him in it. He uses your life for His good purpose, even if your journey started on the wrong foot, hit some bumps along the way, or landed in the ditch - it is not the end of your story. God can use your ditch experience for His glory. God was trying to call me out of the ditch! When Del initially moved into my home, I refused to heed God's gentle warnings. I was out of line in allowing Del to live with me, I knew it, but I ignored it. Del and I were going to be married as soon as his divorce was final and that would square things with God. My intentions were good. Well, we all know what they say about good intentions and what road they pave.

I would not allow myself to acknowledge God's cautionary words. I turned a deaf ear and proceeded to build a life with Del. The two years we lived together before marrying, God's gentle voice visited me from time to time urging me to live holy. Consequently, I really did not have the peace I looked forward to having with Del in those first years. Yet, I forged on and sure enough, when Del's divorce was final we married.

Yes! I was right! After Del and I married, the gentle voice went away. **WISDOM CRIES OUT:** *When the gentle voice stops, that is a red flag!* God can leave us in our foolishness, but I thank Him for His grace. God's grace would not leave me in an unrighteous situation. God's grace would not leave me in the belief that my wrong was right since Del and I were now married. God's grace would not allow me to show men the way, but lose my own way. God's grace showed me I have a heart worth entering heaven. Some would not call what I went through grace, and I would tell them, *"Grace does not always come to the rescue with a soft hand."*

When I realized my actions had hurt someone else, it indeed broke my heart. When I realized how casual we treat God's institute of marriage and how it grieves God's spirit, I knew I had to share my story. When I was at my lowest and cried out to God, *"What did I do?"* - God's grace answered my cry. Really, I must confess, my spirit knew it all the time, but I would not yield to the Spirit so God had to torment the flesh.

Although I have some great memories of Del, and I cannot image being in this world and not loving him, our marriage was not sanctioned by God. When Del and his former wife split up, I interfered and short-circuited the work God wanted to do in Del, so in return, I received from Del what I did not allow God to work out in him. **WISDOM CRIES OUT:** *When God cautions you about something, no matter what you have to lose, cut your losses sooner than later and keep it moving.*

When God started answering and unfolding my life before me, all the pieces, for better or worse, fit together. I had asked God to answer me, I begged Him for answers, now He was on a roll. I was beaten up and exhausted, but God continued, *"I will keep you in the pit, rather than have* **you** *bring a reproach upon My name. What becomes a distant memory to man, I keep record of. When you stand before Me what will be your excuse?"*

That is a chilling question, which many of us will have to answer one day. What will be your excuse (for not living holy)? The world and the church both accept what is displeasing to God. That is why it is imperative that we pour ourselves out, get rid of our ideas, and learn of God for ourselves, develop our own relationship with Him, and He will guide us into *His* truths.

I know things happen and I know some people have some good reasons for divorcing, but the bottom line is we have to do better. The issue is prevalent and not addressed in a manner that is satisfactory to God; otherwise, there would be no need for this book.

This is a tough conversation, and let me tell you, I cringed when I had to write I married a married man. Do you really think Christians want to hear this? Too many of them are divorced and remarried; they do not want to hear their marriage might not be sanctioned in God's eyes! Who does! I am not trying to come down on anyone. Just hang in there with me and keep reading. In some of the following chapters, with God's help, I have flushed this out a bit more; some of you can take a sigh of relief, and some of you have some work to do.

◎✆✇◎

God does not desire for my marriage to Del to end in divorce. He desires repentance and that we understand the magnitude of our offense. I have repented, but that only gets us half way there. If Del does not do the same, sadly, he can never truly be a godly husband to me or anyone else, even if he was the man of my dreams. Folks, this is as real as it gets, it may seem like a tough stance to take, but it really is easy to overcome - all it takes is humility. In repentance, I suffer and in the loss of my marriage, I suffer. On the other hand, in restoration my soul rejoices.

God is serious about marriage and most people do not comprehend just how serious He is. When marriages break down, society breaks down, it causes a trickle-down effect of disorder. This does not fulfill God's will for the world He created and it certainly does not fulfill His decree for godly off springs out of godly marriages (*Mal 2:15*) – which perpetuates a cycle of godly people. Instead, we are perpetuating a cycle of turmoil.

God desires us to live holy before Him. Those who are called by His name do not live as the world lives and those He loves He chastens. I will forever be grateful to God for having mercy on me, even though the rod of discipline has left an indelible scar upon my heart. God's grace and love for me makes it bearable and even worthwhile. God methodically reveals life *His way* to all who have an eye to see and an ear to hear. I will say it again, "*Don't get caught up in your pain and miss the move of God in your life.*" As harsh as it might sound, His plan is greater than your pain.

God had to take me to the breaking point in order for me to receive, in a regenerated heart, what He had told me twenty years earlier. Honestly, as long as I had Del, I might not have ever faced the reality that God was not pleased with me. However, it gives me great joy, even as my heart still grieves the loss of my husband, to know God considered me worth striving for. He did not have to do what He did for me. Maybe He thinks I have a heart worth entering heaven.

❧❧❧

After preaching at my church one Sunday morning, the visiting minister from Staten Island, NY, prayed for people individually. Del and I had only been married for a few years and this was before God called me into ministry. I never forgot what she prayed *into my life*, she whispered in my ear, "*You are highly favored by God.*" Now she might pray this prayer to many people, but I said, "*... prayed into my life.*" Those words stuck with me, they became a part of me because I believed them. **WISDOM CRIES OUT:** *We have the God given power, authority, and responsibility to speak life into people's lives and that is exactly what this minister did.* A seed was planted that begin to germinate; I knew in my heart those words were true. Highly favored, that, my dear hearts, comes with a price.

My dear readers, as long as we are happy and have what we want we take it as a sign God is pleased with us and it is His blessings being poured out on us. How easily we forget – *"He causes His sun to rise on the evil and the good, and sends rain on the righteous and the unrighteous"* (Matt 5:45).

CHAPTER 2
Heartthrob

I met Del while in Phoenix for my cousin's wedding. Out of eight siblings, three younger than me, I was the only one to go on this particular trip with my parents. *Divine destiny was already calling.* We drove all night and arrived at our cousin's house the morning of her daughter's wedding.

Although we arrived early, the house was already bustling with activity. There was not an empty room in the house, joviality and chatter surrounded us. The commotion did not discourage my stepfather from finding a bed to crawl into to catch up on the sleep he had lost driving all night from Modesto to Phoenix. People were coming and going, bridesmaids were squiring around from one room to the next. Giggles and outbreaks of laughter were coming from every direction. The bridesmaids joked and teased while doing one another's hair and makeup. There were several last minute trips to the store to replace stockings that were the wrong size or color, or to get the right lipstick shade, it was one thing after another.

The doorbell was constantly ringing; flowers delivered, food for the after party brought in, and gifts dropped off by friends who would not be attending the big event. The phone was ringing every 5 minutes, one of the bridesmaid's was running late, someone needed directions to the church, someone needed a ride; it was grand central station around there. My mother pitched right in, helping where she could. As for me, I had a ringside seat contently tucked away in the dining room, which was centrally located - all the comings and goings had to pass by me.

13

My mother's cousin, Doris, was a joy to be around. She greeted everyone with a welcoming smile, she laughed easily, instantly making you feel right at home. Although her house was busy with preparations for her daughter's wedding, Doris was still the perfect host. Without a second thought, she warmly opened her home to all who came.

The smell of pressed hair and hot curling irons mingled with the smell of homemade desserts being pulled out of the oven, all floating through the air alerting your senses something special was about to happen. Doris could bake a cake from scratch quicker than, and better than anyone I have yet to meet. While having a conversation with her, she could whip up a cake from scratch and pull it out of the oven before the conversation ended.

Doris became very dear to me, as the years passed we developed a special bond which I cherish to this day. The daughter whose wedding we were attending, twenty-three years later my mother and I would be back in Phoenix attending her funeral. Doris' grief touched me deeply; out of that heartbreaking event, we became friends.

❦

The final hour before the wedding there were a few of us left at the house, everyone else had headed to the church. As calmness settled in the house and we were preparing to leave for the church, our attention fell on this beautiful vision dressed in all white emerging out of a back bedroom. Sadie was smiling, but tears were streaming down her face. Before leaving the house she grew up in, Sadie fell into her mother's arms and wept. The bride was leaving the security of the familiar for what she and her groom must now build for themselves. *God was storing all of these things in my heart.*

The ceremony was lovely, as far as I know it went off without a hitch. The reception was truly a celebration of love. More people attended the reception than the wedding ceremony. The reception hall was packed pass capacity, with people continuing to stream in. Some people were content to maneuver their way through the crowd, get a plate of food, eat it outside, and just hang out. There was no room on the dance floor so people danced where they could. No one came empty-handed; they came with food or drinks, a gift, or huge hugs that suffocated you. Hugs, kisses, and laughter were as plentiful as the food and drinks.

The weather was warm well into the night, which certainly attributed to a larger crowd than expected at the after party held at Doris' house. The dancing continued, food was plentiful, the drinks flowed freely, and the laughter was contagious. I don't know when everyone finally went home, or when I went to bed. From beginning to end, it was a memorable day of love and laughter. It still stands out as one of the best weddings I have ever attended.

My parents planned to stay on a couple of days after the wedding, so I attached myself to my cousin, Reggie (Doris' son), and his girlfriend. They lived together with their three toddlers. We spent the days hanging out with their friends from house to house or cruising throughout the city, or settling down at the park until dusk. When it was time to return home, I knew I wanted to spend the remainder of the summer in Phoenix.

With the help of Reggie and his girlfriend, we talked my mother into letting me stay with him and his young family under the pretense I would be babysitting their children. It was not so far from the truth, although Reggie's girlfriend did not work, I was still a big help. She was a young mother with small children, which is a big responsibility so my help was a welcome break for her. I was so happy to be there I cleaned their apartment (whether it needed it or not) from top to bottom every day.

A couple of days after being at my cousin's place this tall fine looking young man, with a big wavy afro dropped by to visit Reggie, his name was Del. He could not have possibly been at the wedding (or reception) because I know I would not have missed him. I could not take my eyes off him. Whatever falling in love meant at the tender age of fifteen I was completely there, I fell in love with Del the first day I saw him. He was all a girl could want in a guy; good looking, strong, easy going, and although good-natured, he had more of a serious side than the others. Del was too old for me so I lied about my age. We hit it off from the start, talking to him was like breathing, it just came natural. It was as if we had known each other in another life. When Del was around there was no one else in the world - where he was, is where I wanted to be and I positioned myself accordingly.

The summer of '71 was charged with fun, excitement, romantic notions, and growing up too quickly. Del, my cousin, his girlfriend, and a few others made up *our* inner circle of friends. They were the coolest people ever who welcomed me in with no questions asked. As far as I was concerned life was great, there was never a dull moment and every day felt like the weekend. When I was at home around my siblings, being the middle child I was not interested in hanging around my younger siblings and my older siblings had their own lives, which did not include me. Now, there I was hanging out with a crowd older than and cooler than they were - if they could see me now.

When Reggie and his friends got together, sometimes during the week and always on the weekends, we had a ball. They could find humor in anything and could tell the funniest stories about each other. Although I had a lot of energy, I was careful not to show my real age by being a nuisance. I knew how much everyone loved to cruise so when Del would ask what everyone wanted to do, I would quickly say, "*Let's ride*" and off we would go. We would get as many people in a car as we could (in those days you could do that, and the cars were bigger). We would ride for hours, with me always securing a seat next to the driver, Del – I was in heaven.

When Del was around nothing could harm me, I was safe. In my eyes, Del was bigger than life he was my hero. He would never let any harm come to me, let alone be the one to hurt me. As I look back on those days I realize all of Reggie's friends felt that way about me, but at the time no one else mattered, but Del. Life was good and I did not want the summer to end. Starting high school was the last thing on my mind.

Things were going to good to last, my mother got wind (from a little birdie named Doris) of the *extra* company I was keeping and called an immediate halt to it. Doris knew my affections had fallen on Del - *was I that obvious?* My mother did not understand that at the age of fifteen I knew I had fallen in love for the rest my life. Whether Del had reciprocated or not, or knew my plans for *our* future or not, did not matter to me. He was more than my cousin's friend he was going to be my husband one day, I was certain of it, I just needed more time to work things out.

My dear readers, I have been reading your minds every since Del appeared on the scene. The answer to your question is yes, it is possible to fall in love without being intimate. The answer to the other part of your question is no, we were never intimate. I did not know it at the time and probably would not have understood it anyway, but God had placed a seal around me, I was forbidden fruit. God was in control and His purpose (not scandal) would prevail.

Years later when we met again, Del shared with me that something told him not to get out of line with me. He said something was not right. He went on to share with me that although the attraction was there, it just did not feel right so he followed his instinct. Had he not had the good sense to heed his misgivings my life would be an entirely different (unwritten) story. I knew it was not a question of *what* that *something* was that told him not to get out of line, but rather *Who* it was that told him. God dealt with the adult not the child. Sorry folks, but I cannot tickle your fancy with something more shocking or unsavory. When I left Phoenix, my reputation was intact. **WISDOM CRIES OUT:** *Ladies, if you are in a relationship with someone who is pressuring you to have sex, I have two words for you, "drop him." No one should pressure you to do what you do not want to do, and definitely not into doing, what you should not be doing in the first place.*

It did not matter to my mother, whether we had been intimate or not, she was not about to take that chance or any other. The inner circle of new friends were simply too old for me to be around. I pleaded with her to let me stay until the end of the summer. She was not listening to a word I had to say, I was coming home on the first mode of transportation leaving Phoenix. All the pleading and reasoning with her was of no use, she arranged for me to be on a flight back home the next day.

To this day I don't remember if she was at the airport waiting for my flight to arrive only to find out I wasn't on it or if I called her to let her know I *missed* my flight. In any case, I was disobedient and defied my mother's direct orders. Naturally, she thought I had lost my mind. Until then, although sometimes I could be a pistol, I had never challenged her authority.

The following evening after I missed my flight home the doorbell rang at my cousin's place. I jumped up from watching TV ran to the door and without asking who it was, I threw the door open. I thought it was one of our friends. Reggie's house was the hub for visitors; someone was always dropping in to hang out. I regretted that assumption as soon as I saw who was standing on the other side of the door. Lord, I should have asked who it was before opening the door. Better yet, I should have let someone else open the door. It was too late, there would be no turning back, there was nowhere to run nowhere to hide, and I knew better than to try to close the door. There we were face to face my cousin Johnny.

Johnny was my mother's nephew. He and my mother grew up together; he was only six years younger than her. Johnny loved to tell stories and he loved to laugh, he had one of those distinctive laughs that comes roaring up from the belly and cuts through the sound bearer once released. He was a carefree spirit who never cared much about material possessions. He always did his own thing and marched to his own tune. Johnny never stayed in one place too long before he would up and disappear.

Being a mechanic allowed Johnny the freedom to live anywhere he wanted. Therefore, when the travel bug bit, he would disappear without the formality of a good bye. He had no problem being called (by some) the black sheep of the family. I never understood that, I thought every family had a cousin Johnny. He was who he was until the day he left this earth.

Johnny knew Reggie very well; actually, he knew the entire inner circle who I now claimed as my friends. For many years, Johnny lived between Modesto and Phoenix so he had a lot of history with Reggie and his friends.

While Johnny loved to laugh and have a good time, he was not to be taken lightly. He and my mother were crazy about one another. Anytime he needed a place to stay, our home was his home for as long as he wanted to stay. Whenever Johnny did one of his disappearing acts, sometimes up to a year, he would always show up again looking for my mother. He would do anything for my mother. Johnny happened to be around when she needed him and she did not hesitate to send him for me. When I opened Reggie's front door there we were, eyes locked.

Hold that thought for a moment and let me tell you a bit more about little Ms. me.

As I mentioned earlier, I could be a pistol and like Johnny, I was not always to be taken lightly. I could be as stubborn as a mule when backed into a corner. I also had an awful tendency to pick on other kids, I am sure they hated to see me coming. I was well into adulthood when understood why I was such a pain in the behind to other kids. I had that middle child syndrome going on and really did not feel as if I fit in anywhere. There was always a sense of loneliness looming over me.

There was nothing particularly special about me, except that I was the world's biggest tomboy. I could whip any boy and made life miserable for girls (they were too dainty for me, playing with paper dolls, yuck). I was not as cute as my three sisters; everyone always fussed over them and wanted to take them places. As a result, I created my own world. Who knows which came first the chicken or the egg - did I create my own world because I felt left out, or was I left out because I had my own world, go figure. **WISDOM CRIES OUT:** *Young women, never forget that you are, "...fearfully and wonderfully made" (Psm 139:14). The only person you can be is you, so do you well and to the glory of God.*

Long story short, I was a whip, and no stranger to standing my ground. Therefore, God had the right one at the right time in place to deliver me back home. Johnny and I stood there staring at each other; we did not say one word, he and I both knew why he was there. I spun around on my heels, went to the bedroom I was sharing with my small cousins, packed my bags, said my goodbye's and got in the car. I did not speak to him the entire trip home. Ten hours of silence did not bother him one bit, Johnny was on an assignment for my mother, failure was not an option.

Do you believe it! Before we left Phoenix Johnny had the nerve to stop off at a woman's house, for a couple of hours! He reluctantly invited me in and I flatly refused, which was the response he was hoping I would give. I was not happy with him and certainly did not like him very much at the time. He shrugged off my refusal, strutting like a peacock he hurried on to her front door. In the hours he was gone he never once checked on me. He was confident I was not going anywhere and he was right, it was dark and we were a long way from Reggie's place.

Furthermore, I was not about to aggravate him by leaving out of the car. It would not have gone well for me once he caught up with me.

The summer of '71 started with so much fun and dreams of a future with Del ended abruptly in disappointment and a broken heart. What is even worst, I did not get the opportunity to say goodbye to Del. I can now look back on that summer and think about God's word – *"For I know the plans I have for you, plans to prosper you and not to harm you, plans to give you hope and a future"* (Jer 29:11).

CHAPTER 3

Lovesick

How could my mother do such a thing! Having me dragged back home like I was a juvenile delinquent! I had become grown that summer; I knew what I wanted, and was making plans to get it. I was in love with Del and knew he would have done the right thing by me. He could have taken advantage of the situation, but he never did (that had to count for something). Even though he was one cool customer, I knew there was chemistry between the two of us. *The summer of '71 set in motion the path my life was destined to take.*

That summer there was nothing more important to me than being around Del. If we were not taking long drives, or hanging out at a friend's house, there were the picnics at the park (I think blankets and ice chest were as common in the trunk as a spare tire). If Del did not show up at a gathering I was agitated and never gave up hope that he might show up. I was not interested in the long leisurely drives if Del was not coming along. There were the backyard parties on warm nights, attended by a select group of friends. The atmosphere at these warm starry night affairs was very mellow, good food, and good company. None of that mattered to me if Del was not there. If he did arrive, I could exhale. I always managed to be in his space, there was no one else at the party or on planet earth except Del and me. Being next to him was the best place in the world. I was a real chatterbox, it just seemed as though I had so much to tell him. Del would engage in conversation with me or just graciously listen and smile, which was enough for me.

Now, I don't know how they did it, but my cousin along with a few other friends managed to get me into a nightclub! Fortunately, my drink of choice was coca-cola; otherwise, I probably could have pushed the envelope and had a *real* drink. Then again, I did not need anything stronger than a coke, the mere fact that I was in a nightclub was intoxicating enough. I don't know where Del was (he never has cared for nightclubs), but this night he was not missed, the club scene had my complete attention! I have since dubbed that season in my life, "summer madness 1971" - everybody had gone crazy!

When my mother got wind of what was going on she was not happy. She pulled the long arm of a mother's reach from Modesto to Phoenix in the form of Johnny. She snatched me right out of the heat of the madness. When I was deposited back home I did not speak to her for months, I resented her interference. Upon my return home, I went school shopping with the funds she provided, but she was not welcome to come along.

I did not understand until years later how much my behavior must have hurt her. Before going to Phoenix that summer, my mother and I had a good relationship. I was her shadow who followed her around the house imitating everything she did (which to this day has made me a great housekeeper). When she went out for an evening of adult fun, I would watch in pleasant wonderment as she transformed from homemaker, short order cook, maid, chauffeur, and PTA mom, into a hot looking date.

Now, all that had changed, I kept my distance from her as much as possible, she had caused her shadow great pain. At a time when I needed my mother most I pushed her away. I did not share my first day of high school with her and deliberately denied her the pleasure of seeing what I had on (she always liked to see her girls dressed nicely). To think back on those months and the way I treated her makes me sad, she did not deserve my attitude. She never once showed frustration, disappointment, or anger toward me for the way I was behaving instead she rode it out with kindness. She never even confronted me about missing the flight home. **WISDOM CRIES OUT:** *Ladies, you will never have a bigger fan in your corner than your mother. When you turn around and everyone else is gone, she will be right there. She will fight the devil himself for you then must* *turn around and fight you because you do not want her in your business. Until you are of legal age, you are her business.*

My mother was not concerned about how much I loved Del. Certainly she was hurting because I was hurting, but she did what a mother was supposed to do. She trusted me and allowed me to stay in Phoenix and I broke the trust. It was her duty to reel me back in under her direct control and care. She asked no questions, made no apologies, and did not want to hear any excuses. Now as a parent myself I am so proud of and grateful to my mother for what she did for me, she did what was right for her child (and I would do no less if it were my daughters).

❦

I went through my first year of high school in a fog. I could not get into the swing of things, which pretty much set the tone for my high school years. The school had some great athletes who were in the city's newspaper frequently, and our girl's drill team constantly brought home the first place trophy in citywide competitions. I was attending one of the most well known high schools in the city, and I was a lonely lovesick teenager.

By the second year of school, I halfheartedly started participating in the extra curricula activities that teenagers engage in. I hung out with friends after school and on the weekends, but I never felt as though I belonged. I felt like a lonely misfit; in reality, I had gotten a foretaste of adulthood, which I was unprepared for. Nevertheless, Pandora's box was open and I had to find a way to deal with it. I was not only lovesick, but the loneliness I always felt as a child was now compounded. How could anyone understand my pain? In Phoenix for the first time in my life, I fit in somewhere, I mattered, and I felt accepted for me.

It's funny because only in writing this book I'm realizing that my *inner circle* of friends really did not exercise good judgment where I was concerned. For years, my perception has been distorted about the events of that summer and about my new found friends. However, I will always stand by the fact that they were kind to me. They put up with me and watched out for me (even in the club). Furthermore, without making too many excuses for them, the fact is, most twenty to twenty-four year olds still have some growing up to do themselves!

Anyway, when I finally got Del out of my head and became interested in boys, it was never anything serious. I did not allow anyone to get too close, until I met my daughter's father. He was the one for me he was in a word, brash. He was a lot of fun, he loved to party and he was a dresser. It was the super-fly era and he took it to the hilt, he would deck out in the maxi suits and the big rim hats. The color of the suits could be green, red, or purple it did not matter to him because he would hook it up from head to toe. The hat matched the suit and of course the matching alligator shoes. He lived about 50 miles from Modesto and no matter the circumstances: Rain or shine, sick (him or me), only a dollar in his pocket, or gas shortage (waiting in line for hours for gas); every weekend, like clockwork, he was on my parents' doorstep.

After high school and a short stent away at college, we moved in together. He was a fun guy and for the most part, we had a great relationship, we got along well, as we still do. We were young he was not ready for a commitment, I was. After ten years of a lot of fun and one baby, I moved my daughter and myself into our own place. After the breakup something unexpected happened, I started longing for Del. The breakup with my daughter's father opened up the wound of losing Del.

I was with this fun loving guy for ten years, so why was I not grieving this loss, but instead the loss of Del? It just seemed as though life would never be what it should have been without Del. When I left Phoenix the summer evening of '71 it took me a good year to get over missing Del. The first few months after returning home, I suffered tremendously. Grown-ups call it puppy love, well I can tell you this, puppy love hurts like a big dog. Life would never be what a normal teenage life should be. *What was God up to?*

Without anyone telling me, I knew I was in an unhealthy place. I knew, even at such a young age that I had to, somehow, get over Del. Was this what it was like to be in love or was I too young to know how to handle what I was experiencing? I could ask all the questions I wanted to. We can analyze and psychoanalyze what I was going through until the cows come home, all I know is I loved Del and missed him terribly. Subsequently, every time Del would come to mind I would push him out. I would not allow myself to dwell on memories of him and I would not allow myself to fall asleep thinking about him. I am not kidding at fifteen years old I was counting sheep to fall asleep! I did this until I got Del out of my head, but apparently not out of my system.

The months following my departure from Phoenix, I became angry with him because he never came to get me. He did not even try to contact me through my cousin. Del could do anything he was my hero and I knew he had feelings for me. Well what did I really understand? He did not dare risk my mother's wrath. Years later Del and I talked about how that summer played out. He told me about the doubts he could not shake off about me. He had indeed toyed with the idea of coming to Modesto to ask my mother if she would allow him to be in my life. Yet, the more he thought about it, he decided it was not a good idea. He said he never could get pass the thought that something was not adding up (my age sure didn't). Obviously, this was not to be an Elvis and Pricilla Presley story.

❦

I had left the past behind, and was totally committed to the relationship with my daughter's father. Getting over Del was brutal. It hurt too badly for too long to allow myself to fall back into the past. I had moved on and so had he – the night I left Phoenix with Johnny was the last I heard from him. Now I'm in a broken relationship with my daughter's father, although it hurt it did something else, it opened the old wound of losing Del. It brought back feelings I had buried in order to live a normal teen life as best as I could.

After the break up with my daughter's father, my daughter and I settled into our new apartment and new life very nicely. I worked in the office of a high-end department store, which developed my daughter's taste for the finer things. She had become accustomed to getting all of her clothes from this store, complements of my employee discount. If someone gave her something that was not in the store's bag, she would refuse it. However, I had enough department store bags around our tiny apartment to slip whatever someone gave her into one, which did the trick.

When my daughter was four years old, I met my first husband, who was just coming out of a stormy relationship (at least that is what he told me). **WISDOM CRIES OUT:** *Ladies, please, no man on the rebound, whether it is you or him coming out of a relationship. Resist that tantalizing attraction and strong temptation to get involved. Instead, look at the time alone as a gift to reconnect to self. Give yourself the wonderful privilege of meeting you; begin the journey of discovering some wonderful things about yourself. Most importantly, get connected with God. Begin building a solid relationship with God and if it's His will, in His time He will send 'His' man to find you.*

We dated all of six months before his job relocated out of state. You guessed it. No! Tell me you didn't! Yes, I did. I packed up my daughter, packed up our apartment, left family, friends, job, and all we knew and moved out of state to be with him. Crazy, right! Yet, for a whole lot of women this is a familiar scenario. When you are in love, or want to be in love, or think you need a man, you do some foolish stuff. We do stuff that does not make a lick of sense. If someone were to ask you, *"What were you thinking?"* - you would not be able to give an intelligent answer, except, "I was in love." Being in love is not a free ticket to lose your mind! What in the world would make you do something like that? Well, let me try to explain what is going on in a woman's head when we do the irrational in the name of love.

First, and foremost and to be brutally honest, we want a man – what woman doesn't. We want a man for companionship, partnership, for love, marriage, and family, and for some, the need for validation. This alone, as if it were not enough, can cloud otherwise, good judgment. Now, mix that in with the fact that most people accept the good shown to them by other people, and do not look for the bad. We are more inclined to believe what people tell us about themselves, than to not believe it, particularly if a relationship seems to be blossoming. To compound the issue, it does not help if he is cute to boot! He is talking gently, his beautiful brown eyes staring intently at you across a candle lit table and soft music playing in the background... *"STOP! Come up for air! Do not drown in the moment! Breathe! Stay focused!"*

I know your heart is melting, but you have to stay in control. Ladies, keep your head on straight. Disengage and take a few sips of water, not wine. Count to ten and take some deep breaths to get the oxygen flowing to your brain. Really! Does it take all that? You bet it does!

For the simple reason, we all want a good man, we want him to love us, wine and dine us, and the two of you do all the things that people in love do for one another. It has been a long time since a man has been in your life. You probably had given up on any chance of meeting someone. Now, here is Mr. Right sitting across the table. Not only is he pouring his heart out to you, he is hanging on to every word you are saying (someone is actually listening to you). He is giving you the attention that you have not had in a very long time. Complements are flowing generously and it feels good (when's the last time you received a complement from a man). He is opening the car door for you, calling you at the crack of dawn just to be the first one to say good morning to you. Of course, there's dinner that evening, he cannot wait to hear how your day went. When is the last time someone wanted to hear (every detail) about how your day went! Ladies, to use an old tried and true saying, "you have just been swept off your feet," whether intentions are for the good only time will tell.

To be honest, it is a tough spot to be in because it does feel good. When something feels good, it must be right – right? Wrong. Yet, since you are in that feel good place you want more and that is okay, but slow the *more* down. The operative word is *time*, you must give it time – if it is destined to be, it will be in a year or two from now. It is simply not wise to get seriously involved with someone you have only known for a few months. If he is indeed Mr. Right, he will not ask you to do something as drastic as moving in with him (or him with you), let alone as monumental as moving out of state. If he is Mr. Right and you are Ms. Right then the two of you should be able to put your two right heads together and do the right thing by giving yourselves some time.

I don't know of any woman who deliberately start out to have her life turned upside down. Yet, here is the thing, when you looking so hard for love and wanting to feel desired by a man so badly, it makes you an easy target for those with a very different agenda. You can set yourself up to be disappointed by someone who simply has a different agenda than yours, or he's the "love 'em and leave 'em" kind of guy. Yet, he always leaves most of us with something, a baby. Lord, if I can help somebody, I will keep writing!

When I met my first husband, I was not looking for a relationship, let alone a husband. I was not looking, but I was as flattered as all get out when he drove a block pass me at the bus stop then suddenly stopped, without turning around, backed up, stopped in the bus zone, and asked, "Do you need a ride?" "Yes! I still got it!" Satan stroked my ego and it was over, and over it was. The move and the marriage turned out to be a disaster, but God blessed me with another beautiful baby girl.

This baby had the most angelic face this side of heaven, all the nurses drooled over her as soon as they saw her. She was the most serene baby that is until a stranger came near her, tranquility flew out the window. A stranger could not hold her or talk to her without her going into a crying frenzy. However, when we returned to Modesto she took to my family instantly, absolutely no crying spells. What a relief that was.

Although I was totally dedicated to the marriage, it ended faster than it started. You will not believe it, and it took me by surprise, that old familiar pang started to resurface. What was this? What was God trying to tell me? A failed relationships and a failed marriage, Lord as my witness I put my heart into both and wanted it to work out each time. Maybe it just was not in the cards for me to be in a relationship. If I could not have the man I knew (in my soul) I was meant to be with obviously it was neither of these two, maybe I was destined to live the rest of my life alone.

It took some time, but I did arrive at the conclusion that not being in a relationship was actually nice. My babies and I had been through enough. No more men, and no more drama, that suited me just fine! I did not have the energy or the inclination to entertain thoughts of another relationship. I was okay, I was free, old wounds were healing, and I was becoming comfortable with being single. Better yet, I no longer had the aching desire for Del. It was all gone.

That is until my mother and I flew to Phoenix for Sadie's funeral. The first time I met Del is when I attended Sadie's wedding, she would now be the reason Del and I would meet again. Reggie was the same ole Reggie, during the time my mother and I were there he started in on me about Del. He told me Del was living out of state, and although doing well, he and his wife had separated.

Reggie proceeded to fill me in on Del's life since the summer of '71. Well, you know this got me going, talk about flash backs, the feelings I thought were gone all came rushing back. The floodgate was overrun, and I did not stand a chance. Memories I had buried sprung to life bearing fruits of new possibilities. I was hanging on to every word Reggie was saying, but could not process anything beyond struggling to inhale and bearly exhaling. Reggie was laying it on thick finally when he knew he had me hooked he popped the question... *"I have his number do you want me to call him for you?"* My heart was pounding so loud in my ears Reggie's words were muffled. I guess I said yes, because the next thing I heard was Del's voice on the other end of the phone.

He sounded so good; I wanted to go through the phone into his arms. It was as if time had stood still, God had stopped time in the universe just for Del and me. However, one very important thing in time did continue on, I was now of age! Everything I had been through, all Del had been through for life to bring us full circle. This was nothing short of a miracle. I never thought I would see Del again. When returned home the summer of '71, Del went his way and I went mine. Now with failed marriages in both our lives we are on the phone, what were the odds?

I knew Del was married when Reggie made the call; however, Reggie told me Del and his wife were separated. STOP the music: Separated is NOT divorced, *"leave the man alone."* Del did tell me he and his wife were still living in the same house and his departure was imminent. I should have hung up the phone then, but like a fish on a hook, I was helpless. Even if I had wanted to struggle to get loose, the hook was in too deep. We talked for an hour or so and I gave him my number.

Upon my return to Modesto, Del called. We talked and talked, he talked as much as I did. He told me about his failed marriage. I asked if he and his wife had tried a marriage counselor, and recommended that he suggest it to her. I wanted this man with every heartbeat, but I also wanted the right thing for him, yeah right. He told me the marriage was over. Well, folks as you can see I did make the *(feeble)* attempt to help his marriage out. We started making plans to see each other. I could not wait for Del to see me and able to freely relate to me as a grown woman.

Reggie was getting married so Del and I agreed the wedding would be our opportunity to meet up in Phoenix. For whatever reason, Reggie's marriage did not take place, which did not change our plans to see one another. The weeks leading up to the big day when I would see the man of my dreams again felt like months. I did not tell anyone about my plans to see Del. All my family knew is I was going to Phoenix for Reggie's *intimate* wedding ceremony; translation, they were not invited to come along.

CHAPTER 4

Holiness!

I kept my children and myself in church before and after my first marriage ended. Church was important to me and when Del moved in, we attended church regularly as a family. Yes, we were attending church while living together and it was no secret at the church. Please believe me, it was not intended to disrespect God or the church. I simply did not know any better; furthermore, no one pulled me aside to tell me differently. People in the church probably thought I was a brazen hussy flaunting her lifestyle in their faces, which was not the case at all. God whispered in my ear the first day Del moved into my home that it was wrong for us to live together; however, I never made the connection that it might also be a farce to attend church as a family, but not a family.

I was merely exercising my right to make my own choices, without any thought to what others might think. In all sincerity, I was ignorant to my own shame. Yet, it all played out right into God's plan. God did not want me to stop attending church, the plans He had for me would come to fruition through my commitment to the church. With that said, my experience glaringly magnifies the need for babes in Christ to have mature Christian mentors when they join a church. Do not assume when new Christians act contrary to church decorum and/or to God's standards that they are being rebellious or uncaring - because in either case, they very much need guidance from mature brothers and sisters in the congregation.

The lifestyle I was living before becoming a Christian I carried right into the church. In my eyes, it was not a bad life - matter of fact by worldly standards it was a respectable life, one to be proud of. I was doing a commendable job as a responsible hard working single parent of two daughters, who now just happened to be living with a man.

I was raised in the church; consequently, as an adult I never strayed far away for too long before finding my way back. Church was an important part of my life. It took me some time to realize that church was not a part of my life I could compartmentalize. Christianity is not something we don on Sunday and take off Monday-Saturday. I wanted to be in church, I enjoyed church, and I came to understand that Christianity was not a part of my life, but is my life.

I loved the sermons about Jesus as our Savior and Redeemer. God and all His mighty acts in the Old Testament challenged my imagination. Then there was the power of the Holy Spirit, He actually desired to live in me! I believed it, I was excited about it, and I welcomed Him in! God could do great things and I knew He desired great things for me, yet I did not know God as a *holy* God. When you come to understand that God is holy, only then will a true walk with Him begin.

I was active in the church and always strived to do, with excellence, whatever was asked of me. Consequently, when I said yes to God's call to preach, I was one hundred percent on board and at last had a reason to return to school. God was strategically connecting the dots of my life to open my heart to receive some hard truths about my lifestyle in light of His holiness.

About a semester or two away from receiving my BA (which was twelve years into my marriage to Del), I took a *Christian Living* class that would accelerate the demise of my marriage. This class changed my entire outlook on marriage. How I viewed marriage and how the class presented marriage, from God's perspective, was as far apart as the east is from the west. This class opened my eyes to the vital role holy matrimony plays in ensuring a strong spiritually fit society.

It was a rude awakening to realize that too many married people know too little about marriage (which explains the divorce rate). I wanted to share the crucial information I had obtained from my class with them and with couples contemplating marriage. They needed to understand not only the importance of marriage for the survival of a stable and morally strong society, as if that were not enough, but also the spiritual covenant husband and wife enter into with God.

I was on fire and wanted a platform to share what would be new life for dead marriages. Using the example from the book we were reading in class, I proposed to my pastor that we do likewise. I wanted to start an annual marriage service for couples who wanted to renew their marriage vows. They could come every year. The emphasis on the ceremony would be "God is the third person in your marriage." My pastor, who strongly believes in the institute of marriage and will do all he can to counsel couples through a troubled marriage, was in favor of the idea and gave the green light to develop the program.

In my zeal to start up the annual ceremony, satan went on full attack with the first target being my marriage. Even though I was beginning to realize I did not come by it in the right way, I still had to protect my marriage. If not convicted before there was now no doubt I was wrong for interfering in Del's former marriage. With satan on one side and the Holy Spirit on the other, God prepared me to *survive* the battle that I would ultimately lose. I became immersed in His word through various avenues: Bible College, teaching, Bible study, late night studying, preaching and the greatest weapon of all, being a member of the prayer ministry.

The more engrossed I became in my studies, the more I wanted to do right by my marriage and I wanted to help others do the same. I regret the program never started. My marriage was in dire need of attention, this was not the time to go on a crusade to save marriages; first, I had to save my own! I took my eye off the ball, just what satan wanted. **WISDOM CRIES OUT**: *When you undertake to do the work of the Lord, it is not about you anymore, it is about staying focused on the work no matter what satan throws your way. Know that God will keep you, as you take care of His business, He will take care of yours. Del and I should have been the first couple lined up to renew our vows!*

❦

Whether Del was married, whether he was separated or imminent separation, he was off limits. Nevertheless, when he left his wife, I gave him refuge in my home. I should have let him go somewhere else. Not allowing Del to live with me would not have meant I did not love him it simply meant I loved God more. I had a choice to make, God or Del, no matter how unappealing the truth is, I chose Del over God. As a result, I ended up in the middle of something that was not my business. I did not know all the facts about Del's marriage, and I was not supposed to know *any* of the facts, it was none of my business. I had no rights and no opinions, there was absolutely no role for me in Del's dissolving marriage. I came between God's business with Del's marriage.

Yes, I can say what I *should* have done, but since I did not, I want to pass on some sage advice that I pray will be taken to heart by someone. I know all too well, how difficult it is when you love someone and want to be with that person, but when they are already in a (good or bad) relationship, you have to walk away. Only God can say when a marriage is over, you need to stay away from the situation. In someone's struggling marriage, hear me loud and clear, "*Although the marriage may be hanging on the edge, you DO NOT want to be the one to push it over into the dark valley of divorce court.*"

I was a church-going woman and a dedicated church worker at the time Del moved in with my daughters and me. Without anyone's admonishment, in my heart, I knew it was not right to allow Del to live with me. To silence my own conscious and God's gentle warnings, I had several good excuses to *help* God understand why I *had* to do what I was doing. **One)** I could not risk losing Del a second time. **Two)** His marriage was over and he was leaving. **Three)** We were in love and wanted desperately to be together. **Four)** "*Lord, it was You who gave Del back to me after twenty-three years of separation – this is Your will.*"

In response to number one - *I could not risk losing Del a second time.* What God has for you, is for you. "*What He opens no one can shut and what He shuts no one can open*" (Rev 3:7b). In other words, we have to trust God. You cannot lose what you never had; I did not have Del, he currently belonged to someone else – for better or worse, he was married. Furthermore, I did not have him the summer of '71, I was too young.

Listen, we put ourselves in situations God never meant for us to be in. We create scenarios in our own minds, and by any means necessary make it happen and then we want God to bless it. Yet, when we repent, He can certainly use our willful acts to end in a blessing. Lastly, we invite temptation into our lives that we have no control over, let me tell you something satan does not get into the car unless he is going to drive. *"... but each person is tempted when they are dragged away, enticed and baited by his own desire. Then when the illicit desire has conceived, it gives birth to sin; and when sin has run its course, it gives birth to death"* (Jas 1:14-15).

With that said, the truth is I could not risk losing Del; furthermore, I did not trust God to work the events in my favor. I do not know if God would have allowed Del and I to be together or not, and I was not willing to risk it. I played God and blessed myself, but the problem is I could not sustain the blessing.

In response to number two - *His marriage was over and he was leaving anyway.* I know Del well enough to say that if he said he was leaving, then he was leaving. I also now know God well enough to say that if He wanted to change Del's heart toward his wife He could have done so. Never count God out, it may look like the final hour, but divine intervention does not work on the clock. While it is true Del was leaving his wife, I had no right to invite him into my home. How are you going to open up your home to a married man? That was out of order and was foul, even if he/she is not married - the two of you are not married to each other, so in God's eyes it is still out of order. I know a *whole* lot of folks who don't want to hear this (let alone agree with it), but it does not make it any less true or any less foul – it's a stench into His nostrils. If you want to be on God's side, you have to *be* holy. Don't act holy, we got enough actors, but *"...for it is written: Be holy, for I am holy"* (1ˢᵗ Pet 1:16).

When you worship God, you honor Him with a lifestyle that reflects His holiness; otherwise, stop calling yourselves Christians. It is time out for the "it's all about me" attitudes, which do not show the world we as Christians ascribe to a higher standard. As I said earlier, I did not have sense enough to make the connection that I was bringing a reproach upon my testimony as a Christian. I pray churches will seriously start taking some of these new Christians under their wings and showing them *the* "better" way. If they are coming to church, they are teachable, and if they are not teachable, they are deliberately rebellious. It is our Christian duty to make an earnest attempt to find out where their heads are. The stakes are too high.

⟨❧⟩

Del and I do marry and God calls me to preach, so it looks like everything turned out okay for me after all. Now I am living holy, God is pleased with me, and we can now move on, I can preach and serve the Lord with peace of mind. But, wait a minute, not so fast – now that I am in school and studying and mightily preaching God's word, something is happening to me, I am being convicted, spiritually something is amiss. Something is troubling me and it does not take long to realize what it is, my hands are not clean.

You see we do our dirt and if we do not get caught we live like fine up-standing Christians. Let me give you a news flash, absolutely nothing gets pass God. At some point, we have to repent and we have to acknowledge that we left some corpses in our past.

In response to number three - *We were in love and wanted to be together.* We loved each other, could not get enough of each other, and being apart was dreadful. I would count the days until we would be together again. Our love could not see, let alone think beyond one another, there was nothing in the world more important than us being together. We did what we had to do to be together. Our behavior was never questioned by anyone, and honestly, what others might have thought never crossed our minds, it was our world. We did not ask if we were doing the right thing, of course we were - *we* were happy. It never occurred to me that if I really loved Del, I would do what was best for him. I would not allow him (or me) to sin against God.

As we mature in God, we have to start realizing that we do not always get everything we want. We have to arrive at the realization that if we do not have what we most want, then obviously there is a good reason why God has withheld it. We do not give ourselves a fair chance to reason things out because we are resourceful enough to get what we want without God's assistance or approval. Then when we get it, we proudly say, *"Look what God has blessed me with."* God did not have anything to do with it, but we honestly do not see it because we have become masters of manipulation. To get what we want, we have become very skilled at circumventing God's will until we truly do not recognize when it is His will or our own devices (as overt as they might sometimes be).

I was thanking God for bringing Del and I back together, I was telling people, "*Look what God has done, God is good!*" The only difference is, I knew what God had whispered in my ear the first day Del walked into my home, but I was in denial and lying to myself – and what happens, God turns us over to ourselves and we start believing the lie.

We cannot have everything we want and we have to stop manipulating events to get it. We must discipline ourselves to *wait* on the Lord. Paul wrote, "*I have the right to do anything you say, but not everything is beneficial*" *(1st Cor 10:23).* Our lives must line up with the word of God. Just because *we love* someone, the reality is it may not be the one God has for us, or presently the circumstances are just not in our favor. Del and I did not consult God; instead, *we* did what *we* wanted to do because *we* could. Oh, if we would only learn to trust God's will to be done, we would not have to drink the bitter waters of life we draw from our own self-made wells.

In **response to number four** - *God gave Del back to me after twenty-three years of separation:* We do ourselves a disservice when we cannot leave the past in the past, but rather, drag it into our present. "*Forget the former things; do not dwell on the past*" *(Isa 43:18).* We not only cannot forget the past, but some of us live in it. We cannot reach out and get what God is trying to give us because we are too occupied with trying to hold on to what, in reality, we no longer have. Twenty-three years was more than enough time to move on from the summer of '71. I let my cousin stir up in me, what I struggled so many years to turn it into, a sweet memory.

Finally, for the first time since the age of fifteen I was at peace with myself. My life was full and had new meaning: I had my church, my children, my family, a job I enjoyed, I was independent, and enjoying life. After God, I was the captain of my life and my household. In spite of it all, as soon as my cousin started telling me about Del I was not wise enough to put a stop to the conversation. I was captivated with the idea of seeing Del again after twenty-three years. I could not wait to interact with him as an adult and certainly could not wait for him to see the woman I had grown into.

❦

The Spirit would lead us if we would set our minds on spiritual understandings. It should have occurred to me that twenty-three years outside of time is not a speck of dust on the radar of eternity. Divine intervention did not bring Del and I together, it was a meddling cousin (who I love dearly). A life-style of holiness means living in God's truth. Twenty-three years earlier the truth was this man was off limits to me (I was too young) and twenty-three years later he was still off limits (he was married). We must be seekers of God's truth not our own self-serving truth.

I was convinced it was God who brought Del and me together, this was nothing short of a miracle. No one told me what I am about to tell you and there were many who knew my story that could have. In no way am I shifting any blame, I take full responsibility for my decisions. However, I will tell you this, *"Before you make a life altering decision - even if you are convinced it is from God, place it side by side with God's word, and ask yourself, "Does it line up with God's holy word?" If it does not I pray your strength to walk away."*

I did not have to line my actions up with the Word, God told me I was wrong the first day Del stepped foot in my house. I was not strong enough and wise enough to simply place the events in God's hands and allow His will to be done. I was so anxious and caught up in the euphoria that I circumvented godly reasoning and holy living. Hey, I could return to godly reasoning once I secured what was now within my reach.

God hated the way our marriage came about, but He did not break it up (no more than He broke up Del's former marriage). The trouble God allowed to come into my marriage was not to break us up, it was to break us down, and bring us to repentance, not to separation. The trouble came to open our eyes to our wrong so we would, as husband and wife (as one), go to God and ask for forgiveness. To take the first step would have lead us to something else God required, which would be

38

much more courageous than asking for His forgiveness, that was the easy part. God wanted us to acknowledge the pain Del's former wife had felt. He wanted us to feel compelled to apologize to her. When you realize you have done wrong, you should want to apologize. Whether the apology would have been accepted or not, whether we actually contacted her or not was not the point. The sincere desire to do so *was* the point. To have a sorrowful heart and a seared conscious about an offense committed *is* the point. To deeply desire to right a wrong (although you might not be able to) *is* the point.

If we do not stop the degrading acts of bed hopping, marriage hopping, and hurting the people we vow to protect God is going to send a stronger message than this book. When you really think about what repentance is and its intended purpose, an apology is simply part of what the word means. Repentance is a grieving of the heart that deeply regrets something you have done. Repentance means you cannot rest until you have made amends for your wrong. Yes, *your* wrong, own it. Repentance opens your heart to feel the pain that you caused someone else.

Repentance when arrived at, does some serious house cleaning, it cleanses the soul. When you do wrong it does not even matter if you were wronged, you only realize two wrongs do not make a right. You understand just because someone did you wrong, it does not give you the right to return the wrong with one of your own. The Lord says, *"It is mine to avenge; I will repay"* (Deut 32:35). Repentance does not look at the fact that a wrong was committed toward you, it only looks at the fact that *you* did wrong. Repentance is only concerned with your soul, and once right, you can then pray in sincerity for the other person to have a forgiving heart. You pray they will forgive you, not for your sake, but for their own, *"...if you refuse to forgive others their sins, your Father will not forgive your sins"* (Matt 6:15).

Just because we stop being in love – we should never stop treating someone with love. We should never disregard someone's feelings because we do not love them anymore, that is a trick of the enemy. Furthermore, how do you stop loving someone, love is a choice that becomes a commitment – commitment builds character. Good character knows even if you are no longer *in* love, we are still commanded *to* love, which in turn keeps us respectful toward one another.

Someone was deeply hurt and I am not ashamed to tell you, I have felt her pain. I have walked in her shoes. Ladies, we are sisters and we should not be hurting one another, but loving on one another. We should be looking out for one another, not stabbing one another in the heart. Let me tell you something, if you did not get your man under the right circumstances, do not expect to keep him under perfect conditions.

Some rain will fall, and I pray it will fall on this side of heaven, rather than when you must face judgment. Do not lose focus of the topic here, I know trouble comes in every marriage, but I am talking about as a direct result of getting your partner under the wrong conditions. Do not pacify yourself into discounting what I am saying by thinking these are the words of a bitter woman. The words I write do not flow from a bitter heart, but from a contrite spirit.

God's desire was for Del and me to repent, as is His desire for all couples who have gone down some wrong paths. Instead, God ended up using Del to bring me to restoration. Repentance had come for me, but I was not able to move to the restoration phase because I wanted so badly to bring Del with me. You see either Del was going to yield to God's mighty hand or left to his own means. You must understand, we are either going to be used by God or taken captive by our own foolish thoughts, there is no gray area.

The last point I must make about number four, I had no right to bring a man into my home with my children. He could have been the perfect man, but the situation was less than perfect. This is not the message you want to send to your children; whether you have girls or boys, they are both impressionable. Going to church does not make us Christians and it certainly does not make us holy (only a hard-fought for relationship with God can do that). I was going to church and active in the church, but was not living a holy life; furthermore, I did not know there was a difference.

When I truly fell in love with God, the *holy* God, I could now take up where he had left off with connecting the dots of my life. I continue to serve Him, that has not been an option, I did so the last five years before Del left with a heavy heart, and the past two years with a broken heart. Holiness does not come cheap and may cost us what is most dear to us.

CHAPTER 5

Happy Days

If Del could, he would have given me the world. This man loved me and wanted to make me happy. If I mentioned (in passing) I wanted something or showed an interest in something, he would find a way to give it to me. Diamonds, cars, home, clothes, vacations, it did not matter, Del would make a way to fulfill my desires and then revel in the pleasure it gave him to do so. One such instance, our backyard was full of white rocks and fruit trees. The white rocks were an eyesore and the fruit trees were too numerous for us to care for. Del knew the yard was a thorn in my side so while still working, in his spare time, he re-landscaped the yard.

Of course, I was right by his side doing what I could to help. The work took numerous weekends to complete. Although Del never asked for my help at some point, I know he was glad I was as dedicated as he was. It became an all hands on deck project. We recruited help from anyone who had the misfortunate of coming by the house while we were working on the yard. Del was determined to give me the backyard my heart desired, he eventually did and it was beautiful.

After the landscaping, the yard was still rather high maintenance. There was no maintenance done in the winter months and by spring everything was over-grown and it would take several days of intense work to get the yard in shape for the upcoming summer. Del and I would don our yard gear and armed with a bottle of aspirin (for back pain) we went to work.

After the work was complete, we would sink into a couple of patio chairs surveying our work. The sweat and back pain was worth it, the yard would once again be lovely. It was a real sense of pride, and best of all we were ready for summer entertainment.

When there was no project around the house that required our attention, we would slip away for leisurely road trips. Being lost was never a concern, Del could read a map like the back of his hand - he was more reliable than any driving direction website. If we got ourselves turned around (lost), Del would whip out a map, pinpoint our location, and proceed to drive us to our destination.

Among his landscaping and map reading skills, Del is a great cook, if time allowed, he would cook three square meals a day, every day, without a second thought. Each meal was always enough to feed an army and fit for a king. He loved to cook and took great pleasure in others enjoying his meals. Sunday dinners were always at our house and the more people the better. Del held nothing back; from the main meal to trying his hand at scrumptious desserts, the kitchen was his domain. The large meals he prepared guaranteed guest never left empty handed.

For special events, he would pull all nighters in the kitchen. He would be exhausted the actual day of an event, but it was sheer gratification. Del was the super chef and I prided myself on being the super helpmate. He cooked and I prepared the house for guest. After entertaining and the last of the guests were out the door, I would take an hour or so to put the house back in order while Del relaxed. When finished, the two of us would climb the stairs to our bedroom, collapse in each other's arms, falling sound asleep.

❧❧❧

Beautiful roses would bloom in our front and backyard, which awakened in me a wonderful appreciation for flowers. I planted flowers around the outside of the house every year. I never developed the talent for keeping them alive pass a season, but that never deterred me. My love of flowers did not go unnoticed by Del.

Roses and roses by the dozen, the roses were un-ending. Del would shower me with roses, when I returned home from an errand or school there would be roses on the kitchen countertop. He would send exquisite roses to the office; a co-worker asked what my secret was to deserve such outpouring of affection, another co-worker went on line to research a particular type of rose Del had sent!

I thanked God for my husband and I always wanted to be worthy of all the precious things he did for me. We were partners and no matter what we were doing nothing gave me more pleasure than being with Del – I loved being in his space. Life was sweet, I had Del. I was happy and I thought he was too.

CHAPTER 6
Power of the Pen

I have known for a long time that I would write this book, but I was waiting for the perfect ending that I knew God had in store for Del and me. I was prepared to write about our epic love story; a love initially denied, but eventually granted with the lovers being reunited and living happily ever after. I would tell the story of how the lovers repented of the mistakes made in their former marriages. How God not only forgave them, but they were now speaking to couples all around the country about marriage God's way. Yes, the book was going to be filled with our story of love and lose, passion and romance, innocence and disobedience; but, ultimately repentance and restoration.

Well, if we wait for the happy ending in our lives before we do what God tells us to do, we will miss what He has for us and for others through us. We unwittingly put our lives on hold for something that might never happen. Life seldom turns out the way we plan; consequently, life's only real happy ending is knowing we lived obedient unto the Father. Not perfect lives, but faithful lives.

I have been writing every since I can remember. I have always felt the need to write, I was restless if I was not writing. I would have periods when I did not write for months, maybe even as long as a year, but writing, for better or worse is a part of my DNA and I would inevitably pick up the pen again. I have a cornucopia of writings; short stories, poems, poetry, and one other (unpublished) book.

At one point I had become frustrated with writing, nothing was coming together for me. I would start strong on a topic and after four or five pages would take off on a different subject. I would either start from the beginning or go in the direction that I had strayed off on, only to end up at another dead end. What was wrong with me? I knew I could write and I knew I had something to say, so why was I having such a difficult time sticking to one subject? That is exactly why I know this book (and the first one), was inspired by God, the subjects were sure, there was never a dead end or writer's block, instead the words flowed freely and steadily.

As I said at the opening of the chapter, I was not going to write this book until I was living out the ending I had envisioned, so in the meantime I wrote on other topics. Topics that ran out of steam after only a few pages, God was frustrating my plans until I carried out His purpose. Thus, this book came about in a way I never expected via a failed marriage.

Since it was now evident the anticipated happy ending was not going to be the case, I had a tough decision to make and a hard realization to face. Could I write this book in spite of the stunning and shameful demise of my marriage? Would the courage I knew I possessed be strong enough to sustain me to write this book? Yet, what is courage if not acted on at a time when the challenge facing you has the potential to harm you.

Even in this God had to show me it is not about having the courage to tell my story, that's secondary. It is, however, about having the courage to be used by God. As usual, we get it all wrong. We think everything is about us our honor and our desperate need to save face. So of course, the only thing I could think about was the additional shame writing this book would bring. This is the fleshly side of us because my shame (and even my pain) really is not the focus here. Although the storyline is juicy and I have opened up my life to you, do not get so engrossed in my story that you miss God's message. Do not miss the strong admonishment that God is conveying through my story. It is my story true enough, but the message is God's sure enough. So in obedience as His vessel I write.

When God desires to use you (no matter how hurtful or embarrassing it might be), it is to showcase His sovereignty. It is to remind us that no one can usurp His authority or mock His holy standards. God reminds us that He is still from ancient times to now El Roi, the One who sees me. He reminds us that He sees our unholy living, He sees the things we do in secret. El Roi pierces darkness and if He desires to bring your story to light, it is His prerogative. Do you think Rehab was proud of being a prostitute, but her story was for God's glory. You think Jacob wanted millions of people to know he stole his brother's blessings; however, God's purpose overshadowed Jacob's shortcomings.

This Christian walk is not for the faint of heart, when it is time to act on the word of God we must take courage and do what we know in our heart He is asking us to do. God knows our fears and even the disgrace we might have to suffer in the presence of our fellow man, but it does not stop Him from giving us some tough assignments to carry out for His name's sake. So God speaks courage to our hearts, "Be strong and very courageous" (Jos 1:7). "Have I not commanded you? Be strong and courageous. Do not be afraid: do not be discouraged, for the Lord your God will be with you where you go" (Jos 1:9). Life is going to throw us some curve balls, some hard balls, and sometimes we are going to strike out. If we do not give up, but instead push through the difficult times, suddenly our story turns into His glory. It is no longer about the storm or the nightmare that we went through, but it becomes about how God brought us through. Yet, He can only do it if you will "Only, be strong and courageous!" (Jos 1:18b).

As dreadful as it has been for me, God continues to encourage me, so I write. On that terrible night when I needed God to answer my cry, when finally released to get out of bed, I went into my dark bathroom, sat down and began to write. When daybreak came I looked at the words I had written, they were red. In the dark, I had grabbed a red pen. The Holy Spirit said of that red ink, "You will pour your heart out on paper, so write." I was going to write make no mistake about it, but first, and before that night passed, God had to get me to the point where I yield my will to His.

It took some time, but through a number of significant events, mainly Bible College, specifically the Christian Living class, preaching, and definitely, my marriage - God was connecting the dots. He was bringing me face to face with how I truly looked in His sight. Folks, it was not pretty. I had been getting glimpses of how God saw me for a long time, I just refused to stop and take inventory. I did not need to see that person - I had Del. When life was not good and I was sad, I still had Del, and nothing else mattered. Although, I had my priorities mixed up, I never stopped pursuing God and when He allowed me to catch up to Him, He changed my thought process.

Writing this book has given me a new trust in God and a freedom I have not had as an adult. I have had to deal honestly with my integrity, my beliefs, and ask myself the hardest question of all, *"Is God truly the Lord of my life?"* I deeply wanted to write something that would not only make people stop and think, but would make them turn and change. God deeply wanted someone who would write so honestly about marriage that someone just might want to turn around and change.

The road of obedience is hard, it hurts, but knowing something good is flowing out of my mistakes keeps me pushing. Something good is coming out of some hurt I helped to cause in another person's life, whether directly or indirectly, God does not deal in technicalities.

There are a million *me's* in the world, but God chose me to put it on paper. When I get beside myself with sorrow and anxiety, the Comforter speaks one word to me, *"Write."* I could only stand the pain when I was writing. God called out of me what He had placed in my DNA and nurtured throughout the years. Then He used it to tell the world how He feels about His institute of marriage. However, let me be clear, the detours and decisions I made in my life were not all in God's plan, but He used them just the same. He simply incorporates our folly into His purpose. Doesn't that bring in that human element of self-will that usually works against us, but serves to magnify His grace all the more. What a powerful reminder of God's faithfulness when in humility we acknowledge how great is His mercy.

I knew my story could not be told in a 30-minute sermon, but I knew it had to be told. Some people when in pain turn to alcohol, some turn bitter, some turn to the arms of a stranger, I turned to what God had already hardwired in me, the pen. I am not a great writer, but I have a great (although not very complementing) story that needed to be shared. A story of how much God loves me, but more importantly, how much He loves marriages.

Now get this, one of my spiritual gifts is encouragement. I love

48

to encourage others, sometimes all people need is a simple "you can do it" to move into their destiny. I did not know my wrong turns and disobedience would serve to encourage others. This book is not just an admonishment, but also an encouragement to know that God can forgive, heal and restore. If not for the gift of encouragement living inside me (coupled with the desire to write), I do not think God could have used me to tell this story.

When God connects the dots of our scattered lives, it is not all going to be very flattering, but we must be honest enough and courageous enough to embrace it. Only then can we ask ourselves, "*Who is this person God has created and molded me to be, and will I be that person? Do I have the courage to be that person for God's glory and to help bring others into His light?*

God was putting everything about my life in place and then He laid it in front of me. In my assessment I found no discrepancy so He challenged me, He wanted to use my story as His message. God wants to use us. He uses people to touch the lives of other people. The great Strategist was at work, He started me on this path at the age of fifteen and when I look back over the events of my life, I cannot help but see His hand. So I write without the happy ending, yet.

CHAPTER 7
Called!

Seven years into our marriage, I received *the* call. I knew I wanted a closer walk with God, but this was crazy, *"God, are you sure you have the right person?"* Certainly, God was not calling me so I brushed it off as a wrong number. However, God called me again, and again - making it clearer each time that it was Him and He was indeed calling me to preach. There was no mistake about it confirmations were everywhere I turned, so the question became what was I going to do about it? Initially I did not know what to do, but I certainly knew what I was feeling: Inadequate, unprepared, and unworthy.

Inadequate:
Who would want to listen to anything I had to say. I was living an ordinary life with my share of up's and down's. I certainly did not think I had any profound life experiences that would attract an audience. I was going about the business of living and earning a living at a nine to five like everyone else I knew. I was not what you would call charismatic. I definitely was not an eloquent public speaker, nor did I possess the gift of gab. What did I really have to offer?

Unprepared:
What did I know about preaching? How would I go about preparing for such a task? I attended church every Sunday and Bible study on Wednesday nights, I was a *professional* layman. I loved God and desired a

deeper relationship with Him, but it was for my private life not for public ministry. Every now and then, I would take classes at the community college, but again that was for my personal enhancement. Furthermore, becoming a serious college student was not on my list of things to do. My plate was already running over with responsibilities that filled my days, where would I squeeze in school.

Unworthy:

God was entrusting me with not only His sacred Word, but with His people. This was a lofty task, was I worthy of such trust? Could I really live a life that would bring honor to the *high* calling, I know too many preachers that have not and I didn't' want to join the list. I had not lived a perfect life and I had made more than my share of mistakes. How was I going to stand in front of people and tell them how to live when I had not lived so right myself? I could not do it, I may have been called many things in my life, but hypocrite was not going to be one of them.

❦

I was trying to figure it out and at the same time looking for a way out. Some would say I should have sought advice from my pastor or a church leader to help me discern what God was saying to me. I say to them, there will come a time in your life when you know God is speaking to you and you know what He wants from you. You cannot always share with others what God has told you, it must be worked out between God and you. Furthermore, if it really is God, He is quite capable of confirming what He wants without anyone's help.

Oftentimes when you start sharing and soliciting advice, that is when confusion and doubt starts to creep in. This is exactly when too many voices will drown out the voice of God. Too many voices have too many opinions and too many times those opinions are subjective. This gives satan the perfect opportunity to slip in, becoming one of the opinions, usually the most convincing against what God has told you. Consequently, if you do not tell anyone and you end up not heeding God's call, then you only have yourself to kick. Paul said it best, "*But when God, who set me apart from birth and called me, by His grace was pleased to reveal his Son in me so that I might preach him among the Gentiles, I did not consult any man" (Gal 1:15-16).*

Bottom line, I knew it was God and I knew what He wanted, but I was not ready to answer. However, I now had the impetus needed to step up my service. Even though I was active in the church and had various responsibilities, it was time to take a giant step. God was calling me to preach so the need to do more was urgent. I needed to do something that would draw His attention away from what He really wanted. I know I am not the only one who thinks they can bargain with God.

I did the next best thing and started sponsoring women's conferences, which God had placed on my heart to do years earlier. After much planning, I rented a hall, created a full day's program, secured speakers, printed up flyers, and went for it. The day of the event, my mother and sisters were on hand to help, and Del was right there preparing the lunch. In spite of the rain never letting up, twenty-five women pressed their way out and we had a holy ghost filled good time! After that rainy day, I was hosting several conferences a year for the next nine years.

There was no doubt the Holy Spirit was there, the conferences were powerful from start to finish. I had the privilege of witnessing women set free from life-long bondages. God was healing and delivering them from some dark places. Women were flat on their backs on the floor, arms lifted to heaven and crying out. Some wept, while others jumped and shouted, and there were those who merely sat with tears streaming down their cheeks. In the midst of the high emotions, I was carried away to *Psm 56:8* *"You keep track of all my sorrows, You have collected all my tears in your bottle. You have recorded each one in your book."* These were some humbling (and precious) times for me, I was standing in the midst of true praise, and I simply thanked God. It is an honor and a great privilege to be a part of the movement of the Holy Spirit. These women were given a platform to speak; some of their stories were horrific, yet they had the courage to share with a room full of strangers. I know it is because they felt the sincere love of God within those four walls. After years of never disclosing the things they had been through, these brave women dared to step into the light.

Satan had to leave the building because he no longer had a hold on these sisters. They were bringing to light what satan thought he had chained them to in darkness. The Spirit of the Lord was evident; the

53

love was there and the freedom to *just be* cut through the atmosphere. Women who came in burdened and guarded, left laughing and hugging one another and exchanging phone numbers with women they had met only hours earlier. Only the work of the Holy Spirit could have accomplished such amazing events.

Surely, God was pleased with the work I was doing - it was good work and much needed ministry. Yet, I could have sponsored hundreds of conferences, and witnessed hundreds of women released from bondage, I still had to answer *the* call God had placed on me. God was pleased with the conferences and had no problem if I wanted to continue to host them, but it would never take the place of His call. He placed a desire in my heart to do the conferences, but He placed a call on my life to preach. It was clear God was not going to change His mind; consequently, there would be no real peace until I relented. More importantly, I did not know how much longer God was going to put up with my disobedience.

It was time to say yes to God, and when I did the controversy of women preachers was hot on my heels. I was now part of the debate whether I liked it or not. However, I was not going to lose sleep over the issue of women preachers, or pulled into the dispute. Consequently, I decided I was not going to take part in the commotion or let it hinder me. I had to concentrate on my yes not on some people's no. The call was big enough I could not allow the disagreement to be a distraction. Anyway, with or without my input the debate was going to continue for a long time to come. My decision to say yes to God was strictly between Him and me. I am not going to live apologizing to man, for saying yes to God. Since it was God's invitation I accepted, I fully expected Him to keep me in His peace as far as this particular topic was concerned.

Once I yielded to the call, the fire ignited within me. If I was going to be a torch, I wanted to be equipped, so I enrolled in school. Throughout my college years, I had the privilege of studying under some awesome professors, some of whom did not believe women should be in the pulpit. Their beliefs did not affect me, or my studies in any way, nor did it diminish the respect I had for them. These dedicated men and women are truly the unsung champions of God's word, no matter what their stance is on women in the pulpit. Besides, the issue of women in the pulpit will be settled, once for all, soon enough.

Talk about a leap of faith, I was actually returning to school as a full time student with a set goal. The Bible College I initially attended was a sixty-mile round trip commute from my home. Classes were every Saturday morning into the early afternoon. As expected, Del was as patient and understanding as always. He never once complained or showed signs of disapproval about me accepting God's call or returning to school. My Saturdays were school days, along with some week nights spent engrossed in homework.

When I transferred to a college practically in my backyard, classes were Saturdays and one to two week nights, and homework was now nightly. During the school year, Del and I would steal away for some long weekends and even managed an entire week's vacation away for his birthday.

Before and after graduating with a BA in Christian Studies, I had numerous opportunities to preach. I must confess that the call I had initially fled from became very intriguing, God was using me in ways I never thought possible. I had to ask myself, *"Who is that woman preaching?"* I did not know this person and I certainly did not have any control over her. **WISDOM CRIES OUT:** *When God desires to use you, most likely, it is the person in you, you never knew existed.*

To study God's word and to have the privilege of sharing it is nothing short of humbling. Every time I delve into the Word, I learn something new about God and about myself. When you can attain some measure of spiritual insight, you can honestly relate to the man who said, *"...I was blind, but now I see!"* (Jhn 9:25b). I had been there – blind to all my foolish ways, but now I could see, so I thought. Unknown to me I was still partially blind, but because of His grace, God would not leave me there.

God was giving me spiritual insight a little at a time, which I could have only attained by being a student of the Word and preaching the Word. As I mentioned in the Holiness chapter, God was preparing me to accept and confront the ugly truth about my own life. God will go to great lengths to prepare us to truly be worthy of such a great and costly salvation; and to be a herald of His word too, He will dismantle every part of your life and lay it before you. As I said earlier, it is up to us to accept it and embrace it. God does not work on the clock, He takes His time in preparing us for real service.

◎☙☙❧◎

Real service is "come what may," you stay the course. Real service even when thrown into the fire or into the lion's den you will not turn back or step aside. Real service means staying committed in the tough times, unfair times, unappreciated times, the lonely times, and yes, the discredited times. Real service will test you, stretch you, grow you, and ultimately satisfy you.

God called me into real service by way of preaching, but there was so much more involved. When I said yes to the call, God had a work to do on me, in me, and I might add, *for* me, *before* He could (truly) work through me. God knew exactly when it was time to turn up the heat, exactly at a time when my heart was most tender (while studying His word) and at the most precious time in my life (during my marriage). I was beginning to see life through spiritual lens and sincere gratitude for God was filling my heart. I was learning so much about Him and my heart was becoming tender in a new and different way. The soil of my heart was fertile and ready for God to drop a word into and it would take root.

I gave you my reasons for consistently resisting God's call: Unprepared, inadequate, and unworthy. Although I was well into preaching, I was on point with one of my concerns, but for the wrong reasons. When you began to understand what it is truly like to walk in God's light, realizing that before then you were in darkness, it is quite a revelation. You want the world to know, with God, all things are possible, and preaching allowed me to do just that. Then Del left and unworthiness came in. Was this a test? How could God expect me to continue to preach? Was I worthy? Now that the blinders were off and I received in my heart what God told me that night I cried out, how could I continue to preach?

For a while, I tried to preach through it and I tried to continue with my duties at the church, but I was dogged by too many emotions. I had to somehow sort it out, I had to get my head and my heart aligned! I desperately wanted to be in right standing with God. Was I a home wrecker, would Del had gone back to his wife had it not been for me? Maybe, maybe not, but that really is not the point; the fact is, I was wrong and there is no wiggling out of that. Consequently, was I worthy or was it a trick of the devil? Y'all, I was doing my best to understand what God was doing in me and what He was trying to bring out of me.

He was doing something not to harm me, but to give me a lived out and lived through testimony. I had to remember God's promises, that He would not fail me; and as bad as it was for me, I could not fail Him. God was using me and I had to allow Him to have His way. Even under fire and the feeling of unworthiness gnawing at me, I had accepted the Call, so no matter the circumstances, God had prepared me for real service; turning back was not an option. Then it came back to me, what He told me that long dark night when I called on Him, *"I have plans for you and what you did does not negate those plans. You are being held accountable for your indiscretion and purified of your offense while fulfilling those plans."*

CHAPTER 8

I Care

Someone I dearly love commented to me that I was tough as nails. I am not sure if it was meant to be a complement or not, but it was her take on how I was dealing with Del's departure. Another friend, whom I have known for many years, told me I was just too calm and collected for someone who was going through such a tough ordeal. She proceeded to tell me she could never suffer the breakup of her marriage without crying on every shoulder she encountered.

The comments did not surprise me, I did *appear* too nonchalant, especially to those who knew how I felt about Del. I was going on with life as if my world was still right side up. I was composed (on the outside) and had not deviated one iota from my normal routine. Furthermore, whenever Del's name came up in my presence I would not so much as raise an eyebrow. As a result, I can see how I came across to some as being a strong woman and to others as being indifferent about the breakup of my marriage. However, the reality is, no matter how much pain we are in, life goes on.

When the wind is knocked out of us life does not stop or even slow down to give us a chance to catch our breath. Instead, we must pull double duty of maintaining our daily obligations and graciously carrying our pain. What people have to remember, they are on the outside looking in and are privy only to what you want them to know. Let me tell you, a whole lot of praying goes on for just a little strength to make it through what feels like an endless day (let's not even talk about the nights). You take it one day at a time and at the end of each day give God an exhausted, but grateful thank you, while at the same time not looking forward to the next day.

I did care; however, I did not trust myself to detour from my daily routine. Besides, I did not want to make my broken marriage the topic of every conversation. For months, I was careful not to show any outward signs of sorrow. I put my head up and marched through it. It served no purpose to put my pain on display - the shame was bad enough.

I cared. From the day Del and I united I started planning our future, and after twenty years a significant milestone was coming to fruition, Del was retiring. He had paid his dues and was leaving the workforce. It was now his time to do whatever he wanted to do. I knew Del would continue to be an early riser, which would make it easier for me to roll out of bed and still go to work. I could look forward to him being in the kitchen brewing coffee and starting breakfast. I did not tell my co-workers about Del's retirement, I wanted to surprise them when he started dropping by the office. Then there would be the times he would be out of town. I knew I would miss him, so I had to prepare myself for the days when Del would be visiting his family or at the lake house for long lazy days of fishing and grilling. I was more excited about Del's retirement than he was.

Well, so much for my big ideas on how his retirement would play out, let alone kick off. Without one word to me, immediately after retiring, Del took off out of town. I was sorely disappointed that he did not give me the opportunity to celebrate his retirement. To boot, his birthday was days after his retirement, so we had a double celebration, but it was not to be. It was such a letdown for me and for my family, they were all on standby ready to support me in whatever celebratory plans I had for Del. He had not been talking to me for months, but I still wanted to acknowledge his retirement and his birthday. It was the right thing to do, we were still living in the same house and I still wanted to be his wife.

I cared and my mind was flooded with memories that choked me to tears. I cared that we had painted the inside of our home together, I painted the walls from the floor up to as high as I could reach and Del painted from where I left off to the ceiling. We always worked in perfect harmony, sometimes without saying a word (this was a different silence than the silent treatment). I cared that he built the brick wall in our backyard, which took hundreds of heavy bricks. As the wall progressed, Del was moving further away from his supply of bricks, so I lugged them to him to reserve his energy for laying the bricks only. I knew he was tired, so was I; nevertheless, I was determined to work as long as he did. I took pride in being his faithful helpmate.

I cared that he had secretly planned our tenth year wedding anniversary getaway. Del's instructions to me were to inform my professors of my absence and pack for four days of nice weather. We drove to Phoenix, spending the first night with our sister-in-law, whose company I absolutely love. The next morning we headed for beautiful San Diego! We spent a couple of nights at a cute little hotel and had dinner at a fabulous steakhouse. Before returning to the hotel, Del let me do some shopping. He patiently hung out with me while I took my time going through racks of clothes and trying on numerous pairs of shoes. As I shopped, he stood nearby watching me in total contentment and love.

Headed back home, we took the scenic route, Pacific Coast highway! I love the drive, but I never ask to take this particular route because it adds a significant amount of time to our travel. The houses along the way are something to see, floor to ceiling window-paned homes perched on hillsides overlooking the ocean, with patios wrapping around, what looks like, the entire house. The views leading up to the ocean drive are breathtaking. Winding roads lined with huge majestic trees that seem to touch the sky. Just when you think the view could not get any prettier, the forest is left behind and you are riding alongside the Pacific Ocean, simply gorgeous! Although the day was overcast and a bit chilly, with jackets on and pants legs rolled up, people were strolling the shoreline.

As great as the scenery was, the real treat was seeing and experiencing the places that Del had been. All along the way he pointed out places that his job had taken him. This gave me a glimpse into his world, some of the places he had been and the delightful discoveries he had found were impressive.

After hours of driving and sightseeing, I was in for another treat. In Monterey, Del took me to one of the popular seafood restaurants in town; the service was genuine hospitality and the food was worth the drive. We did some sight-seeing and spent the night. We headed for home the next morning, but Del had one more surprise, he turned me loose in another one of his discoveries, an outdoor mall some miles outside of Monterey. Del hates to go shopping with me, but once again, he patiently kept up with me while I popped in and out of stores fussing over what I would buy.

It was obvious he had done his homework for our anniversary getaway. Del was a man with a plan and he executed it with heartfelt precision. He was like a big kid beaming with pride as he shared with me his life on the road, and I loved him for that. Wining and dining me the entire time, he was a sweetheart from start to finish. The word "no" was never in his vocabulary and impatience never stood a chance with him. He was totally committed to ensuring that I had a good time, it was indeed all about me. I talked about that trip for months, I am sure some people were tired of hearing about it. We had some great times on other trips, but this one was perfect from start to finish. It was an act of love on Del's part and a time out of our daily routines to show gratitude for our lives together.

I cared and I would assure Del it was those simple pleasures that I treasured and looked forward to sharing with him for the rest of our lives. I never stopped believing that Del would eventually realize how much his behavior was hurting us. There was no way he was going to let me go, he loved me, at some point he was going to snap out of whatever it was that was eating at him, I just knew it.

⁕

When I look back on those last years, I can see even if Del wanted to concede, he had reached the point of no return. He had painted himself into a corner that he was either unable to or unwilling to come out of. I like to believe that in his heart, Del knew he had behaved badly toward me. I could be wrong, but knowing he had behaved badly, Del was not willing to risk me refusing any attempt he might have made for reconciliation. I still cared and frankly, refusal was not an option, had I refused, Del would not have tried a second time. Furthermore, any refusal on my part would have given him an excuse to snub any future attempts I might have tried for reconciliation.

It was like playing chess, every move I made although carefully thought out, was always the wrong one. While I may have been justifiably upset with Del, I did not have the luxury of playing the role of the delicate flower unjustly wounded. Whatever his advancement toward me, I would have accepted it, but Del never tried.

I cared, but basically it was Del's world and you either found a fit in it or you did not. He was not going to go out of his way to invite you in or to explain himself. That might seem harsh to some, it was for me, until God started revealing some things that helped me to understand Del better, not totally, but better. It bears repeating, so I said it again in the Baggage chapter, *we have to look beyond the walls that people sometimes build around themselves.* I cared, but Del just would not allow me to be his better half.

When you love someone you do not exploit their vulnerabilities, you protect them. If we would take the time to look beyond ourselves, if we would stop thinking that everything is about us, God would allow us to see others clearer. I have my faults and weaknesses, but Del made up for them, and actually complimented them, he was my better half. I thought he loved me so much more for my weaknesses, instead, it seemed to be my strengths that he could not digest.

I would get crazy angry with Del because he would not let me in, he would not let me help us! When I get to that boiling point, I admit I will not only throw a fit, but anything I get my hands on. Checkmate! When I blew up it was the wrong move, then it was not about his behavior, but about my very bad behavior. I could not win. What's more, Del would not allow himself to look beyond my acts of rage to see they were only because I cared.

I cared about Del and I cared about our marriage, I was in love with our marriage. I wanted our marriage to be good, but the harder I tried the wider the chasm between us became. I never would have betrayed Del and contrary to what some might think, this book is not a betrayal. It is time out for the superficial stuff. I am praying for a healing of marriages. Too many marriages are hurting; people get up in the morning, get dressed, before leaving the house put on their happy face to meet the world, all the while dying inside. The most important part of their life is a mess, hidden behind a fake smile.

63

I attended a women's conference in Palm Springs, CA years ago, one of the speakers said to an audience of over 5,000 women, *"If any of you have been married for more than five years you know what satan's abode looks like."* The crowd went wild! Women all over the building were clapping, stomping, shouting, and giving each other high fives in agreement! Obviously, they could relate to what the speaker was saying. This one sentence brought down the house. So, who is this book betraying? You might currently be living in paradise with your spouse, but you probably had to go through some storms to get there. For those of you who have had paradise throughout your marriage, *"God bless you."*

What I went through is bigger than me and bigger than Del. On this fragile journey, God has kept me for all these years for a reason. This is for a healing of people and their marriages. This is for those who have separated or divorced, I say to you, *"It is not too late. God can still heal, forgive, restore and yes, even reunite, if that is your heartfelt desire."*

God waits to pick up the broken pieces of our lives to shape them into what He has purposed them to be. If you are married, God ordained it to be good. Even if you came about it in the wrong way, have to go through the pit to keep it, the good is waiting for you, do not give up, and for heaven sake, do not stop caring. God wants to restore your marriage.

Come on ladies and gentlemen, what really is your understanding of marriage? The Bible clearly states, *"Has not the one God made you? You belong to Him in body and spirit. And what does He seek? Godly offspring. So be on your guard, and do not be unfaithful to the wife of your youth"* (Mal 2:15). Marriage produces Godly offspring. God brought husband and wife together to populate the earth with godly people who will honor Him from generation to generation.

Marriage is the most intimate and scared union on earth and if we do not take that most seriously, what does that say about who God really is to us? How do we expect to produce children who will reverence the Lord and have the courage to obey and trust Him in the face of adversity, when we cannot do it? What kind of resolve will they have to hang in there when things get tough in their lives, when we cannot do it in our own lives?

You bet I care, there is too much at stake not to. Whether I will remain married, I do not know, but I do know this, I will always care not only about my marriage, but also about all marriages.

CHAPTER 9

Anger

I was distressed, humiliated, and just plan ole dumbfounded. For the life of me, I could not figure it out let alone come to terms with Del walking away from our marriage. How could he disgrace me before my family and friends? To tell the truth I was ashamed before God. Everyone knew our fairy tale love story. What were the odds of us coming together after twenty-three years of separation, two thousand miles between us, almost a ten-year age difference, and both of us (in my case, had been) in other marriages. People knew how crazy Del and I were about each other. How could I rationalize what was now happening? We were in love, we wanted to be with one another, and nothing else mattered or was given consideration.

When Del's divorce was final, we married. Del and I were on our way to marital bliss nurtured in Christ. There was no earthly reason why our marriage would not last, but there sure was a spiritual one. We were in church, had Christian pre-marital counseling, and married in the church, but the seed of our marriage was not planted in Christ, although I sure tried to water it in Him. Folks, if we want the blessings of Christ in our lives we must plant spiritual seeds. Nevertheless, not everything has to be lost and life does not have to beat us down because we go astray or did not know any better at the time. God is a forgiving God who lavishes His grace on us. He is a God of second and third and many chances. When we mess up God wants to forgive us, He waits for the day when we take responsibility for our sins and repent, and start planting seeds in the right soil.

I was humiliated and left trying to make sense out of Del's behavior. Yes, we started wrong, but when I took responsibility for that wrong I was prepared to suffer the consequences; that is, as long as I had Del at my side. Well, Del not only did not offer any comfort in my punishment, it turns out he would be my punishment. I thought I could deal with whatever I had coming, but not Del's betrayal. As hard as it was, as unbelievable as it was, I had to reap the seed that I had sown. Sin is a boomerang and we never know when or how it will return from whence it came. I had been hurting for a long time, but when Del walked out I was inundated with all the emotions I had kept in check for so long.

Shock, denial, sadness, confusion, anger, bitterness, shame, unworthiness, and rejection were all in line to become my new best friend. In the late hours of the night, sadness and loneliness wanted to share the vacant spot in my bed left by Del. On countless mornings while driving to work, bitterness and rejection wanted to hitch a ride. Then there was enough - I could not avoid or hide from it. Enough showed up everywhere I went. The person staring back at me in the mirror was no longer enough. I was not good enough or understanding enough; falling short of enough was constantly nipping at my ankles. Yet, most dangerous was not caring. Try taking that attitude to church; it was a prelude to blatant defiance, "*Lord, why should I praise you when you have allowed my private life to become a public charade?*" Not caring makes you foolishly bold because you figure you have nothing to lose. Surely, you do risk losing God's patience; there is an end to long-suffering.

For those of you who know what I am talking about, you know how vulnerable a hurting heart can be. There are two things the heart intuitively seek out, comfort in the pain and a defense against the shame. The emotions have to come – they are a part of the excruciating process that eventually brings a healing. You will become stuck on a particular emotion longer than you should, and the longer you hang on to it, the harder it is to shake it. For better or worse (usually worse) this is the one that has become your comfort in the pain and your defense against the shame. Although all the emotions serve a purpose in the healing process, please understand that most of them or negative, all of them should be temporary, and none should take up permanent resident.

The emotion that yelled the loudest, clawed the hardest to take center stage in my heart was anger. Anger did not want to be a one-night stand, but desired a long-term relationship. Anger whispered in my ear, assuring me that I was justified in choosing it. Sure enough after weighing in on some of anger's benefits, I decided that anger was exactly what I needed. Anger would be a great asset, a shield to deflect the shame while also keeping the bitter sting of betrayal at bay. Yes, anger was looking like a good place to hang my hat for a while and best of all, it gave me a free pass to be spiteful toward Del. I could treat him exactly how he deserved to be treated and no one would blame me; furthermore, there would be those who would happily cheer me on. **WISDOM CRIES OUT:** *When operating out of spitefulness be careful of those who cheer you on. You need a friend right now, but not one who will only tell you what will make you feel good, or worse, encourage ungodly behavior. You have made your share of mistakes do not compound it by giving back evil for evil. Stick close to people who will love on you, pray for you, and for your estranged mate.*

Taking on the role of the indignant victim was very tempting and had a lot of potential. I could play the role of the woman scorned to the hilt. In the last weeks before Del moved, I could have made it very difficult for him by being a real pain in the-you- know-where. I could have hastened his move, yet I let him move out at his own pace. By this time he had retired and had ample time to move a lot quicker than he did. Yet, I never bothered him or was unkind to him in any way during those final days.

Del's move was a slow and agonizing process. Each day I returned home from work he would be there, which gave me a glimmer of hope that maybe he had changed his mind. The hope was short lived, I would walk by a closet or countertop, back up, do a double take, only to realize that something (else) was missing. While at work, I had to push the thoughts of what was going on at home out of my head. I had to stay focused, keep my composure, and do my job. My home was in a shamble and there I was at work, but what else could I do – it was obvious I was losing my husband; I could not lose my job too.

My sisters, I love y'all because I know what you would have said, "*If you're leaving then get to stepping. Get a U-Haul truck, back it up, get all your stuff, put it in the truck, boy bye!*" Yet, I did not say a word because that was just Del, he was in his own world and I will say it again, you fit in his world or you do not. Six months after Del's departure I attended a wonderfully uplifting women's retreat. I actually dropped my shoulders and took a deep breath – I did not know something so simple could feel so good. The retreat was just what the doctor ordered, until I returned home that Sunday afternoon. Del had been to the house and taken some more of his things. It upset me terribly, and just like that, the wonderful just-what-the-doctor-ordered weekend was swept away clean. Talk about killing me softly, it was a painful move, but when you think about it, what is a painless way to leave your wife?

After Del left, in anger I could have changed the locks on the door, threw his mail in the garbage, and sold all his tools. My attitude could have gone all the way south. That is precisely why it is best that we get through some emotions as quickly as possible. It may sound like an oxymoron, but the negative emotions are intended to be healthy releases; so, if you are angry, let it rip. Who wouldn't be angry! Rant and rave, and then get over it. Everyday make a conscious decision and earnest effort to get over it. Everyday, make a conscious decision to let it go, until it is gone. Holding on to the negativity leads to bitterness.

Bitterness is a by-product of any negative emotion or negative experience that we cannot get pass. You cannot control other people's actions, even when their actions are causing your pain. You have to fight to keep yourself in a spiritually and mentally healthy place. I was not going to allow anger to manipulate me. As hurtful as betrayal is and as hard as it kicks you in the gut, it cannot be the pitiful excuse for becoming an angry woman and certainly not a bitter one. **WIDSOM CRIES OUT:** *We have choices and as terrible as life can be sometimes, as unjust as it can be at times, nothing justifies taking the low road.* From time to time, anger would rear its ugly head, but it was not welcome to stay (at least not for very long).

You could have parked a truck between us, up until the last night before moving out I still allowed Del to share ~~our~~ my bed. He was always careful to stay as close as possible to the edge of the bed on one side and I was careful to do the same on the opposite side. Two people whose world was once each other were now worlds apart. It was a crime scene with satan's fingerprints all over it. Satan was having a field day. He was the strong man in the house, prancing around by day as if he paid the mortgage, and at night resting comfortably in bed between us.

The cold hard distance that can grow between two people that share the same house is chilling. You work hard to build a home that was once your safe haven has now turned into a battleground. Do not get it wrong, the battle does not have to always be a physical one or slinging verbal insults; the blows are just as devastating when talking to one another has ceased. The common courtesy of a simple *"good morning"* or *"hello"* requires herculean strength. This is a familiar scene for many marriages; it goes on every day in thousands of homes across America and around the world. A husband and wife, who could not stand to be apart for a day, now cannot stand to be in the same room for an hour.

So what happens? There are those who throw in the towel and walk away, which is a cowardly act, just as it is cowardly to stay and treat one another badly. I can tell you this from first-hand experience, *"Your behavior grieves God terribly and disappoints heaven greatly."* You will hear me say it repeatedly throughout this book, *God loves marriages* and what God loves heaven cheers for; heaven is cheering for us, yet we throw the fight and hand satan the victory. You must realize what God loves satan hates. Satan will use the power we unwittingly give him to shipwreck our lives.

We throw the fight because to fight somehow makes us feel weak or needy, we forget that God says, *"He is made strong in our weakness"* (2nd Cor 12:9). We feel strong when we say; *"I don't need you and if you want to go, then go,"* that is a cheap shot. When the marriage goes too far left, yet one of you can still show kindness and a desire to move the marriage to a better place, that's strength. When the temperature in your home is below zero, but you can still say to your mate in sincerity, *"I love you and I'm committed to our marriage,"* that's maturity.

That uncomfortable feeling of weakness and neediness that we refuse to give in to and adamantly deny we are feeling is humility. Humility is not a trait respected in our society, sadly not even in the church. How unfortunate it is that we have missed this essential character building quality. There are great blessings in humility. Humility is the fertile soil God uses to mature and raise up those who are willing to bow down. It takes strength (and is indeed a beautiful act of humility) to admit that we need our spouse and that the mere thought of losing them makes us ill.

Few people are willing to fight to keep what they fought so hard to get, specifically, their spouse, and most importantly, their vow to God. No one wants to be the one to put them self out there with the possibility of being rejected. Rejection is hurtful, it is a hard blow to the ego, and there lies the gridlock. For the sake of my marriage, I placed my ego in God's hands, only then was I able to put myself on the line. When rejected, I choose not to take it personally, although that was my first inclination; however, my ego was in safe hands. I was rejected, even betrayed, and in this fleshly tent, it messed with my mind and made me question my self-worth. Yet, I could not let the sting of rejection cloud my thinking. I knew I had done the right thing and I was going to be okay. Consequently, when anger courted me, I had to keep all the self-doubt and bruised ego junk satan was trying to fill me up with in perspective.

You must have an unwavering sense of who you are and Whose you are to put yourself out there to risk rejection; otherwise, you simply will not do it. I put myself out there; my pride and my heart as beat up as they already were. I risked it repeatedly for the survival of my marriage. I prayed that Del would see that the enemy was satan not me.

It is not that I was handling everything perfectly or even right, I made more than my share of mistakes. The difference is I was searching for solutions and I was committed; bottom line, it was not about Del, or me, but about our marriage. God wanted humility and repentance, satan wanted pride and destruction.

May I just preach for a moment, just bear with me and let me get this off my chest. *Lay your pride down or your marriage will fail or it will not be a good one (which is still failure). You must look at one another over the walls of self-preservation that we build around ourselves, and see the need. Stop for a while, step back and refocus to see the person you first fell in love with. Do what God does every single day for us; look beyond our faults and see our needs, and love us in spite of our many shortcomings. Pick your marriage up off the ground and hold it in the highest regard possible. No one marries with intentions of making their spouse miserable, saying and doing hurtful things that crush the spirit. Somehow we lose our way, and the marriage goes astray and creates hurt feelings and hard feelings, but folks, we got to get pass that – we have to do better by the person we vowed to cherish. Marriage vows are kept in the good times, but are to be binding in the bad times. In the rough times, remain respectful toward one another, remain kind toward one another – move gently and speak softly.*

I will let you in on a little secret of how satan works. As soon as you make that public declaration to *"love and honor, for better or worse, until death do you part"* to one another; it's game on! No way is satan going to let you make good on that public vow. All bets are off, and he is coming at you with everything he has. Satan is going to attack you on every side and nothing is off limits. To name a few, your values, your wallet, your health, your weight, and your very identity are going to come under attack. Heaven help you if you bring children from another marriage or relationship into the marriage, which is more ammunition for the enemy, actually, that is TNT! The sad thing about it, satan continues to use the same old tired bag of tricks, but why would he change his game plan when it still works.

Satan is a trickster who we have a hard time recognizing because he relies on our lack of knowledge of him and sadly, our lack of knowledge of the ways of God. Perfect example: The person we once loved and would have died for, we now hate and want to see dead. Why? Because we are self-absorbed people, who think it is all about us. When problems are encountered, we take it personal, which is exactly what satan relies on; otherwise, he has no power. Scripture tells us *"...don't think of yourself more highly than you ought to think..."* (Rom 12:3). We do the opposite of what God tells us - which again, is what satan counts on.

Here is the real deal, marriage exposes the real you to the one you vowed your undying love to and the real you is not always pretty. That is okay, in life, we are continually evolving and different experiences bring out the good and/or the bad in our personalities. When your negative behavior is pointed out by your better half, please refrain from using it as a bone of contention in your marriage. Instead, turn everything over to God He specializes in turning negatives into positives! There is only one side in a marriage, God's side. Yet, in the heat of life the battle lines become blurred and our marriage turns into two hostile camps both based under the same roof, and guess what, "...*a house is divided against itself, will not stand*" *(Matt 12:25).*

If I did not initiate a conversation with Del, there was none. What a change from the times we talked until falling asleep in one another's arms. I knew satan's tricks and I was not falling for them, so I became the great initiator. In the last four years of our marriage everything Del and I did together was due to me initiating it. "*Honey, you want to go out to dinner?*" He did not leap at the invite, but he would go. "*Honey, you want to go to the lake, oh come on, you're not doing anything else. I'll drive and you just relax.*" After some cajoling, he would finally give in. As the years passed, his hesitant yeses became fewer and fewer, until he just refused my invites, there was no amount of pleading or persuading to change his mind.

Eighteen years into our marriage, and Del leaves. How does one justify such behavior? Is there anyone he can be held accountable to? Was not a crime of some kind committed? How can he get away with this? There was no recourse, no comfort, no satisfaction, only humiliation. Who could argue with anger wanting center stage or trying to steal the spotlight every opportunity presented!

❦

My mother was crazy about her son-in-law and you could not tell her anything negative about him. When Del and I knew we would be starting a life together, to my surprise, he asked my mother for my hand in marriage. At that time, I was well pass the age of needing my mother's permission to marry, but he honored her, and totally flattered her by asking. How big do you think that went over with her? How many of her friends do you think she told? This gracious act created a special bond between Del and my mother that endeared Del to her. Chivalry emerges out of a generation where the word morality means little, respect for self and others means less than little, you welcome courtesy with open arms.

We live in a world where rude, cocky, egotistical, and coarse behavior is commonplace. When displayed, good manners will always be praiseworthy. My mother took notice, she fell in love with Del and everyone else in my family followed suit. Both our families looked upon our marriage with pleasure. What would make Del feel like he had to leave a place where he was loved and respected? Yes, anger was itching to move in.

❦

In our marriage I constantly referred to God - His standards were my measuring rod. It is God's standards that we are to live by and when there is a disagreement in the marriage, God has the final word; therefore, neither one of us had reason to feel slighted. Marriage has so much potential to do so much good. Our churches need more examples of godly marriages. Children and young adults desperately need exposure to godly marriages. Del and I had the potential to be one of those examples; it angered and disappointed me that the privilege was taken away. It was a great opportunity to show that although we started wrong, with repentance, God restores.

Anger would try to latch on to me, even before Del left in anger I would tell myself to move on and forget about him. Anger could indeed mask the hurt I was feeling. Anger warned me never to trust anyone with my heart again. Anger could harden my heart to Del, to the shattered dreams, to the misinformed gossipers, and even to considering never doing ministry work again. I was just done with it all. All the reasons to be angry were valid and lined up; however, did that give me a right to be angry?

My foundation was pulled from under me and there was not a thing I could do about it, that made angry! There were days I wanted to sleep through; it made me angry because I couldn't! There were days I wanted to stay in the long term parking garage with windows rolled up inhaling the toxic fumes of anger. I was angry with Del, but angrier with myself - I messed up royally. I didn't listen to God.

I had to fight through all the junk to see the enemy. It was satan, he wanted me to stay in that desolate place of anger. By now, if you have not learned anything else about me, you should know that I hate to give satan the victory. Yes, I went through my season of anger, a wonderful marriage with the man of my dreams was over, just as a puff of smoke vanishes in thin air - gone. Was it really just a fairy tale gone bad?

I did everything within my power to make my marriage work. I had paid my dues in the relationship department and I was entitled to a happy marriage. With a closer walk with God, I was maturing and knew what it took to be happy and I had earned the happy ending, yet I was unhappy, and anger wanted to be the one to act it out.

My dear readers, happiness has nothing to do with this Christian walk. Do not go legalistic on me; Christians are not walking around with their heads dragging on the ground because they are not supposed to be happy. God is not so much concerned about our happiness, as He is about our holiness. I will tell you like my sister-in law once told me, "*You have eternity to be happy, but only a lifetime to be holy.*" My brothers and sisters, we need to strive for holiness. God said, "*be holy…*" (1*st* Pet 1:16), not "be happy" – be holy because I am holy. God is looking for the pure not the corrupt; too many people become corrupt chasing happiness. Happiness only fulfills fleshly desires, which are temporary. Ask God for the joy of the Lord to come into your heart. Joy will keep you when happiness eludes you. Furthermore, I have lived long enough to learn that there is indeed happiness in this Christian walk, but will only be realized when living life God's way.

At any rate, the anger stage did not last - oh, it comes and goes but is never welcome to stay. I was hurting, but I had to deal with the pain with a heart of flesh. I thank God He never answered my prayers to harden my heart. My job was to stand up under the pain and not try to get rid of it through wrong avenues.

Restoration does not come cheap, and it certainly does not come through anger. I did not answer the question, a few paragraphs up, "*did I have a right to be angry?*" Anger is a natural emotion, which we all experience. Yes, we have a right to be angry, but we do not have a right to become anger. Anger becomes hard and unruly, and inevitably, without warning, turn on innocent people.

CHAPTER 10
Divorce Papers

Three weeks after Del left the heartache was still fresh. However, on this particular evening something else was going on inside me that took precedence over the pain. I could have laughed up a storm and at the same time cried a river of tears. If I did not know any better, I would have diagnosed my behavior as being in the first stage of a breakdown. Yet, something else was going on; the atmosphere was shifting around me.

I had been through a lot, which could only be described as a one sided knock-down, drag-out fight to keep my marriage, only to lose it. I knew all too well the spiritual reasons for the trouble in my marriage; all the same, I felt heavy. Well, I said to myself, "*What's done is done, at some point you have to stop crying over spilled milk and pray for strength to move on.*" Moreover, do not ask, "*Could it get any worse?*" We all know the answer to that one, it can and it did.

I really did not know how to react or what to feel; what is the appropriate reaction when served with divorce papers? I wanted to cry and at the same time I wanted to laugh - I could do neither. My stomach was unsettled as was my soul and I had a keen sense of movement around me (but, I was alone in my bedroom). When I held those papers in my hands something about the spirit in me was familiar, yet nothing that I could recall ever experiencing before. My spirit was stirring, as in all earnestness I begin to realize the battle I was in. I knew at that moment, not only was the Holy Spirit stirring in me, but He was also hovering over me and what's more, heaven was watching! "*Well, I'll just be, satan*

77

is trying to take me out - he most truly hates me," I said to myself. Yet, satan can never hate me more than God loves me! Satan can never do anything to me that God cannot deliver me out of!

I could clearly see the spiritual battle satan had waged against me. God allowed me to see just how badly satan wanted to destroy me. The second I held those divorce papers in my hands, I knew I was at a crossroad. Even though I was hurting, I was also feeling somewhat special and in all humility, I knew I was on heaven's stage. How many times, if ever in this life are we privy to a supernatural fracas, taking place, at the exact moment it is happening! I was there, satan was there, and the Holy Spirit was there too! I was an awe struck witness, who was also the main character!

I will not deny it my heart was burdened down to the floor (which is our flesh) while at the same time my spirit was lifted up to the throne room (our spirit man). I was disheartened when I received those papers, but God gave me something that made all the difference in the world - spiritual insight. The divorce papers were to be satan's deadliest blow to turn me away from God's purpose.

When I received those papers it hit me in the center of my being not just how much satan hates me, but how afraid he is of me. I do not say that to brag because he would be afraid of us all, if we all had the courage to be God's vessels. We all know satan's plans for us, this is Bible study 101 – *"Satan comes only to steal, kill, and destroy"* (Jhn 10:10). Satan's work was all over those divorce papers, I almost could not stand to touch them! I had been getting glimpses of him all along the way in the demise of my marriage, but he would never fully show himself, I would call him out, but part of his trickery is to lurk in the shadows. To keep us off guard and off his trail; satan comes out of hiding plants seeds of lies, division, and discord then crawls back under cover. Just when you think you recognize him or have put your finger on him as the source of your problem, he slides back undercover, leaving you to second-guess yourself.

You must understand spiritual warfare, you are either for God and doing things in a way that honors Him, or you are not, there is no neutral ground (as some would like to think). I will say it again, as I have and will continue to do so throughout this book because you have to get it. *"God did not want my marriage to end, He wanted repentance from both parties. The one God did not get repentance from, is the one that would be used to destroy the marriage."*

God wanted to place our marriage on the solid foundation of His forgiveness. But! God forgives when forgiveness is requested, and it can only be requested when you realize you have done something wrong. Furthermore, you can only accept that you have done something wrong when you can look at your actions through the eyes of God.

WISDOM CRIES OUT: *When you start viewing life through your spiritual lens and not the physical, it places you on an entirely different playing field. The spiritual is more real than the physical, the spiritual is more powerful than the physical, and the spiritual eternally outlast the physical. Until we recognize these facts, we will never understand spiritual warfare. "For our struggle is not against flesh and blood, but against the rulers, against the authorities, against the powers of this dark world and against the spiritual forces of evil in the heavenly realms" (Eph 6:12).*

Satan hated me while Del was still in the house. I had the nerve to continue to extend my hand of friendship to Del. I had the nerve to refuse what satan was so cleverly trying to offer me after Del left, another man (that trick worked before, but not again). Del did not leave our church after leaving me, I had the nerve to continue attending the same church, with my head held up (even though I was feeling down inside). Then I had the unmitigated gull to think I was going to write a book about it! As far as satan was concerned, that was the last straw! Satan wanted to stop me and divorce would do the trick. Being walked out on was bad enough, to tell the world I was also being divorced, I would not have the nerve to go through with it.

Satan was right, if it had been me, it most certainly would have been the end of it. If it were me, I would have pulled down the shades and had a pity party a long time ago. If it were me, I would have found some comfort in a few glasses of wine every night. If it were me, I would have accepted a strong shoulder (if you know what I mean) to cry on in the midnight hours. However, it was not me, it was the Jesus in me - the fight was His not mine.

When Del left, I was determined to pick up the pieces of my life, a huge part of that meant writing this book. Satan was incensed so he circled back to finish me off, but God said not so. The moment those divorce papers were in my hand the atmosphere shifted. My emotions and the movement around me that I was trying to understand, was God moving in and taking control of the fight! *"No weapon formed against you shall prosper (Isa 54:17),"* if! you get out of the way and let God fight your battles!

God revealed my foe, which confirmed the suspicions I had been having for a very long time, but either feared to face or reasoned it could not possibly be. You see, it is the same when you are not sure it is satan undermining your works, as it is when you do not want to face that it is him. In either case, it gives satan the advantage. He will nip at you and run for cover until he becomes bolder and starts taking chunks out of you until he devours you. Understand this, satan takes great pleasure in taunting you and goes to great lengths to ruin you before he strikes the fatal blow.

Well, that underhanded trick with the divorce papers only served to validate I was doing what God wanted me to do. When things get tough, do not turn back. Be strong and keep pushing and praying – you have to stay the course and see what the end is going to bring. Satan wanted to silence me, in silence we suffer, and in silence a piece of us dies every day. I will not be silenced by the enemy, I have a story to tell that is not mine alone, but so many other's - who need to know God's truth. No matter how badly my story started or how terribly wrong it ended, satan does not get the victory.

The evening I received the divorce papers, it was unexpected, yet not surprising. After the Holy Spirit confirmed it was the archenemy, I allowed everything that had transpired to sink in. The next couple of hours I went about my chores and prepared myself dinner, even though I really did not have much of an appetite. I moved about, in what seemed like a surreal evening, but it was all real. It was another stage in the breakup to overcome; I had to keep breathing, consider the source, and stay focused. I begin to realize the calmness in me and around me, the movement had stopped and peace was resting on me. Sounds very much like the night I called on God and He showed up. God was keeping me every step of the way.

When I settled down for the night, a frightening thought came to me. If not for paying attention to and heeding the Holy Spirit, I could

80

have fallen for satan's trickery. I could have fallen for the Father of all lies and let those divorce papers make me act a fool. I could have started calling folks to tell them what a rotten thing Del had did and how spiteful he was being. I could have shot him off a couple of nasty text messages. On the other hand, I could have had a pity party, crawled into bed at eight o'clock in the evening and cried myself to sleep. Or, I could have reverted to what I used to do on more nights than I care to recall when Del was still living at home, walk the floor in the middle of the night trying to figure it out.

We must stop allowing *our* emotions, *our* feelings, *our* self-righteousness, and *our* pain to control us! Pay attention to what God is trying to do; how God is trying to direct you, mold you to make you an over-comer of the problems that threaten to take you down! After what I had just experienced earlier that evening I was not about to give satan the satisfaction of me striking out, crying it out or even trying to figure it out. Number one, I was tired of crying; two) folks get tired of hearing your sad story (even if it is juicy – at some point all the juice is squeezed out); three) you can go crazy trying to figure out why people do what they do, and most importantly; four) God showed up!

All the churching, all the schooling, the Bible studies, the teaching, the women conferences, the preaching, and Lord, all the praying - what was it all for! What was the point of it all if I was not going to apply it when I needed it the most? "*Do not merely listen to the word, and so deceive yourselves. Do what it says*" (Jam 1:22). Bless those who have the courage and faith in God to apply His word to their lives when their back is up against the wall.

Why would I give satan anything that might resemble a victory for him? I just could not do it; furthermore, as I had already resolved when Del left, I closed the door of my home to satan. I closed the front door, so he tried to come in the backdoor! Close all doors, windows and seal the cracks; otherwise, he will find a way in.

Obedience to God's word and walking in His purpose for your life takes courage. Writing this book took every ounce of courage I could muster up. God is okay with that, He honors the courage it takes for us to do the hard stuff that He ask of us. Step out, He will protect you, "*Only be strong and courageous!*"(Josh 1:18b).

The harder it is to do what God wants us to do, the greater the importance we do it, the greater His glory, and the greater the opposition. I will not try to mislead you, doing what God ask of us is hard, period. The opposition looks like giants, but take courage, with one stone God can take down the Goliath's in your life. So with divorce papers in hand I started thanking God and praising Him. It took all my strength to push through the hurt and summon up my own words; there I was, faced with the obligation to put into practice what I preach.

Too many times, I had stood before the congregation on a Sunday morning preaching, "*I don't care what you are going through, that's right it does not matter what it is or what it looks like, God still gets the glory. Your break through is in your praise! Praise God, in spite of how you are feeling...*"

The remainder of the night I praised God until I got tired. I knew I was in a fight and I was not going to lie down in defeat. God had showed up, He revealed satan and his plan, and He supernaturally immersed me in His Spirit. How could I turn back when He so graciously provided what I needed to go forward? It is important to God that I be strong and courageous no matter the obstacles.

By bedtime, I was exhausted and elated all at the same time. I was sad, but happy. I was alone, but not alone. I reviewed the contents of the papers, placed them back in the envelope and never looked at them again. I did not show up for any of the court dates mailed to me, but went to work instead. For me the battle was over.

CHAPTER 11

Baggage

I knew firsthand the pain of a failed relationship; however, you take your chances when you let someone into your heart. Nevertheless, I did not want to carelessly put myself in that position again. I was brutally honest with Del about what I did not want in a relationship. There was no guessing or reading between the lines, 'I did not want drama.' Of course, we would have our differences, that is to be expected when people share the same space. However, the chances of any drama or drawn out differences were slim, Del and I were both too old and too tired for such none sense. We were mature enough to agree to disagree and agree to keep it moving.

I felt obliged to put my cards on the table before Del and I merged households. I told him I was coming into our union with a positive attitude and an open mind. I assured him that I was happily leaving the past where it belonged, behind me.

Leave your baggage behind; you will not need it any longer. It is a new day, the old has passed away. Take a deep breath, say your prayers, and allow yourself to trust again. I can hear some of you now, *"Yeah right, she sure can tell other people what they should do. It took some time and a whole lot of heartache to collect all this stuff, and now she's suggesting it be left behind, just like that?"* I know all too well how difficult it is to leave *your stuff.* The thought of letting go of the things that have become the trusted gatekeeper of your heart is a scary proposition. However, if you desire a healthy relationship you must give up what you feel is your right to carry old baggage into a new relationship. Because one thing for sure if you bring the baggage in, at some point you will unpack it.

Baggage is unchecked issues that sabotage and ultimately destroy relationships that otherwise have a chance of being lasting and good. Baggage comes from all socio-economic backgrounds, we have all had our share, but at some point, we must resolve to rid ourselves of the load. I understand that most of us cannot just drop the baggage as if it never existed. How do you forget the stabbing pain that the unsuspecting act of betrayal caused by the very one you entrusted your heart too? How do you forget the hurtful words spewed at you from the same mouth that promised to cherish you? Eyes that once lit up with pleasure every time you came into his presence, now shoot daggers at you from across the room. How do you forget, but more importantly, how do you forgive those who have tried to kill you spiritually, psychologically, and physically?

Oh no, you must never forget – to forget would leave you vulnerable; to let your guard down would be a stupid thing to do. You trusted and betrayal was your payment. This time you are wiser, you are smarter, and you are equipped; you now have some protection, and no one will ever hurt you again – you have baggage.

As justified as you may be in lugging around baggage filled with hurt and mistrust in one compartment, and an arsenal of defensive weapons in another, it is more detrimental than all the hurt you have endured. You are dragging a heavy load that only slows down and sometimes brings to a halt the beautiful plans that God has for you. What you have gone through is not a coincident. It was not to kill you, nor to harden you, but to bring you to a purpose that extends beyond you. I will say it again, *"God's purposes are bigger than our pain."* He will use one to touch one or thousands, we just do not know.

There are some safe places you can go to begin the tedious process of unpacking baggage, if not in a counselor's office and/or a pastor's office, then definitely at God's altar. Unpack all the junk, all the bitterness and brokenness: Broken dreams, broken promises, broken heart. Unpack the disappointments, the abuse, the fears, and the lies, unpack it all before

84

God. Tell Him about each hurt as you carefully pull it out and hesitantly unfold it before Him. With trembling hands lay each disappointment at His feet. Pull out the balled up crumpled past of molestation as a child that, in disgrace, you hurriedly stuffed down to the very bottom of the bag. As tears of shame spill off your cheeks pull out the abuse inflicted on you by someone you trusted - that same abuse you now inflict on others who trust you. Give it to God, as you break down and weep in the sad realization that you even packed someone else's stuff in your baggage, carrying it around and claiming it as your own.

My goodness! You have a lot of junk; half of it you can't even recall where it came from or know if it's yours or someone else's. Listen to me, at some point it must no longer matter where all the stuff came from, it is time to rid yourself of it. Unpack the weapons you have collected over the years, weapons wired to detonate if your mate unknowingly pushes a wrong button. Give it all to God. Cry out to Him to give you the strength and courage to leave the baggage with Him, never to pick it up again. He will not judge you, or penalize you. God understands that we all carry some deep battle scars, usually from friendly fire. In great anticipation, God is waiting, He says, "Come to me, all who are tired from carrying heavy loads, and I will give you rest" (Matt 11:28).

As time goes on our baggage gets heavier because if we do not get rid of it, we will find a reason to add to it. Folks cannot figure out why they are always tired, sick, friendless, miserable, unhappy, and always mad about something. They fail to make the connection that it is the toxic baggage. The first step toward unpacking is to recognize that these unhealthy behaviors are tools devised to turn on you not to protect you. Tools that will drive people away, these trusted gatekeepers are not to guard your heart, but to harden it.

Some would argue that the unhealthy behavior is not to drive loved ones away. You would be correct, because I do not believe it is what the person's intent really is; nevertheless, it certainly is the end result. Depending on how attached you are to your baggage, if you don't drive a loved one away, you will pick up your baggage and run away, especially if your mate wants to take a look inside! You are not willing to let anyone in, and you are not willing to let go.

Consequently, we unpack our baggage on unsuspecting people. You desperately want to be in a relationship, you even get married, but never let on that you have sneaked some baggage into the love nest. You tell yourself it's okay, "*I will just hide the bag in the room no one ever uses.*" As soon as trouble rears its head, you remember your baggage. Although the situation is not serious enough to warrant unpacking anything, it sure is a comfort to know that your backup is nearby.

Notice what happens, your defenses are now on high alert, your guard is up and ready to detect and act on the next presumed *assault*. That is exactly how people with baggage behave, conscious of it or not, they are always prepared to defend their space.

We have all heard the term "the honeymoon is over." At some point in a marriage (six to twelve months), the honeymoon phase of the marriage ends. With hard work and the willingness from both parties, the marriage can come full circle, returning to the honeymoon stage for the duration of the marriage. This honeymoon will be the best; it has endured the trials that come with building a trusting and loving union. This honeymoon is one of appreciation, respect, and a heartfelt delight in one another.

However, it is the in-between-time when you have to roll up your sleeves, put fragile feelings aside, forget about the baggage, and go to work. You have to get down to the serious business of building a marriage with strong walls that will stand on the God ordained foundation of your marriage vows. These walls will be built out of disagreements and compromise, mistakes, forgiveness, tears and laughter, and surrendering of self for a commitment to each other and to God. The walls are built of genuine admiration, trust, and love for one another.

It is the in-between time that the struggle of the merging of two (not just physically, but more importantly, spiritually) into one takes place. This critical time is when we run the greatest risk of unpacking our baggage. Each bump the relationship hits, each misunderstanding that must be addressed, and it is this time in the marriage when you are most at risk for complicating an already delicate process. It is at this very juncture in the marriage when our true colors start to surface. This most critical and fragile time of the marriage is when you run the highest risk of hitting a bump you can't get over. Consequently, you go in that dark room where you put away your baggage, and you proceed to unpack.

I can tell you with a high degree of certainty once you start unpacking, you will not stop until the suitcase is empty. The issue that sent you running to unpack a weapon becomes secondary to the behavior you are now displaying. In one fell swoop, you lock and load, take aim and fire. Your spouse must be thinking a stranger just ambushed them!

When you bring baggage into the marriage, you wreck havoc on an unsuspecting spouse, who probably is not equipped to deal with your baggage. Your spouse is not your psychiatrist or your antagonist, they are people who fell in love with you and married you to be your partner.

∞∞∞

Here I thought I was one of the lucky ones. Pastors all over America on any Sunday morning expounding from the pulpit, "You women, you so desperate for a man, you go out and get the first man who looks your way. You bring him into your house (he was living with his momma), you bring him around your children (he don't visit his own children), let him drive your car (he don't have one), and you let him eat you out of house and home (he's always hungry). You talking about y'all in love and going to get married (you don't even know if he's divorced). What is wrong with y'all – you that hard up for a man, you'll take any man? You clean him up, bring him to church and three or four Sundays later he's missing, what happened? Or worse! You marry him! He don't come to church, then you stop coming to church, a year later you back at church, going through a divorce, and he's nowhere to be found. You have to learn to wait on God!"

Ladies, we have heard this speech more times than we can count. It always somehow work its way into the preacher's sermon. The danger is when we hear the same thing so many times, we tend to make light of it or turn a deaf ear, doing either one will not dismiss the truth of it.

I was so proud because that sermon did not apply to me. I had a good man, a Christian man, a hard worker who could pay his way and mine too, and to top it off, he cooked. Women would ask me all the time if

Del had a brother or an uncle. I was humbled by Del's love for me and generosity toward me, he was too good to be true, it took twenty years, but it turned out to be exactly that, too good to be true.

Unknown to me, he did not leave his baggage behind, as I pledged to him in the beginning of our relationship I would. When I think back on it, although I made that solemn pledge to him, he never returned the favor. My dear sisters, when we want what we want and when we think we have it, we throw caution to the wind. Even when we think we are playing it safe, we are deceiving ourselves and trying to convince God. For the simple reason, in the beginning there are usually telltale signs, and sometimes, dead giveaways that we either ignore or tell ourselves, "*That will never happen to me, it's different with him and me. He loves me.*"

⚬♋♌⚬

Del placed me on a pedestal, and I was comfortable there and feeling on top of the world, I was safe and secure. I worked, but with his income, I had some financial freedom to do what I wanted to do – shop. Although I had a few household bills that I was responsible for, I always had something left over to go shopping.

I love to shop, and when the relationship started going downhill, shopping became a blessing (and could have become a curse). I would shop for me, my grandbabies, the house, the car, the yard, the church, it did not matter I just needed to shop. I was a shopping maniac; after work, I headed to the mall. If I did not have a commitment on the weekend, I was at the mall (or another get away place that I will talk about later). I knew it was crazy, but knowing it was not enough to stop me. I was out of control, something had to give, and it did.

One evening, after work, I was in a department store eagerly contemplating what I was going to buy, when without warning, I was disoriented. I could not move for what seemed like a very long time, but in reality, was probably only seconds. When I snapped out of it, I wondered around the store picking things up but not really looking at what it was. Why was I there, what did I want? I certainly did not need anything.

I left the store without one bag (which was out of character). Sitting in my car, I tried to figure out what had happened to me. I looked in the mirror to see if my mouth was twisted, maybe I had suffered a stroke. It did not take long for the answer to come.

Right there in the store, the Holy Spirit touched me and I was instantly, burnt out on shopping. I had to face what I did not want to acknowledge. Shopping did not ease the pain or change the fact that my marriage was slipping away; thus, there was no reason to shop myself into the poor house. Shopping was becoming my baggage (figuratively and literally) and could have landed me in financial bondage. However, no matter how much I shopped, I still faithfully and cheerfully gave my tithes; I am certain that was my saving grace. I never went so far out on a limb that I neglected my financial responsibilities to my church or my household.

I had to face the fact, shopping was a pain suppressant, not a cure. Shopping only dulled the pain and delayed the inevitable, returning home to a cold house where the main characters did not talk to one another. I would return home with bags and bags of *stuff*. Yet, there was not enough *stuff* I could buy to fill a house void of love. Shopping could not ease the pain of a failing marriage.

❦

I was secure in our marriage, even when it was bad. I thought Del felt secure as well, apparently not to the extent of forgetting about the baggage he had brought in. How could it be that he never truly trusted me, we were good together, we did everything together, and we enjoyed being in each other's company. He would go to the grocery store and stroll down every single aisle. I did not care for grocery shopping, but went along just to be with him. I was content to wait in the car snoozing or reading a book until he finished his leisurely shopping trip.

I really cannot say what the bump in the road was in our marriage that sent Del to that dark room where he secretly started unpacking his baggage. Year after year he unpacked until finally everything was out. We all know once you unpack something it is next to impossible to neatly put it back as it was. Once it is out, you have to deal with it, you have to find a way to slay the dragon(s) for good or it will devour everything around you. I mentioned it earlier, if the behavior displayed does not send your loved one running, then the one who unpacked will eventually pick up their baggage and leave – which is exactly what Del did.

How do I know this was baggage and not something our relationship created? That is not only an excellent question, but also a fair one. Ladies, we could learn a lot about a man if we would pay close attention to what he is saying in the beginning of the relationship. In the beginning is when there is more talking and information freely given by a man than he will probably disclose in the next twenty years of your life together. Rarely do men repeat or harp on what they share, they are just not wired that way, so get it while it's hot off the press, after that it's yesterday's news. The beginning of a relationship is prime time for information gathering. If something said causes your antennae to go up, do not brush it off.

Del disclosed a lot about himself in those first few months of our relationship; however, I was gazing into those beautiful hazel eyes and listening with my heart and not my brain. It was years later when I started to replay those early conversations in my head. When I started putting the pieces together, it was too late. At that point, my marriage was already in the crisis stage, the only thing I could do was damage control.

Ladies, get the information first, and then gaze into his eyes. As you gather information, take some time alone cozy up with the Holy Spirit, play back the conversations, and ask God to help you sort through them. Share the conversations with a trusted friend who can objectively help you analyze them. There is no such thing as being too cautious - this is *your* life! Live it based on wisdom, not on feelings. You are looking for a long-term relationship, with the hope of marriage, so you want to make a rational decision based on as much information as possible. Furthermore, it works both ways – men, you should be doing the same thing.

I had baggage, but I made the decision to leave it. I was looking forward to a new life with Del. I felt like God had given me a new lease on life and I was grateful. When Del and I started off, he made it clear that he wanted a fifty-fifty relationship. Shoots! We had to go find Teddy Pendergrass' song, "Fifty-fifty Love." That was our theme song. I thought I knew what Del wanted based on a song! How crazy is that!

The last five years proved impossible, it was a no win situation. I could do nothing to keep Del content, let alone happy. The baggage was unpacked and the weapons stayed loaded and cocked. I was giving seventy-five percent, ninety percent of the time and in the last three years; I was giving ninety percent, one hundred percent of the time. The last year, I gave one hundred percent, one hundred percent the time – Del just stopped. What happened to the fifty-fifty he was so adamant about in the beginning? What did a fifty-fifty relationship really mean to him? Ops, I guess I should have asked that question in the beginning of the relationship when he was open to talking. This was important to him, and I missed the "prime time" to dig deeper because I assumed I knew.

It was in the beginning when Del talked about a fifty-fifty relationship being important to him. In the beginning of the relationship, life was wonderful and fifty-fifty was an obtainable goal. The reality is, it is not always going to be good times then what does fifty-fifty mean? Hey, when times are good you can do the entire one hundred percent by yourself, that's easy! It is not so easy when things are not going well, that is when knowing expectations is vital, and if one does not hold up their end, what are the consequences. It takes two to make a marriage successful. **WISDOM CRIES OUT:** *Contrary to popular belief, it only takes one to destroy it. If both parties are not committed, the marriage cannot survive.*

I was on board, I was determined to do my part and his too if necessary, and it became very necessary. I was doing my fifty percent and Del's, if you do the math, certainly that would equal one hundred percent to give us a viable marriage. However, that is not God's math, nor was it Del's. Number one, God expects effort from both parties, He is even willing to accept one doing more, when the other one is incapable, *not* unwilling. Number two, I was not doing Del any favor by shouldering his half of the commitment, he was not impressed or flattered by my efforts and it only prolonged the inevitable. Poor guy, as I look back, I can say he probably stayed as long as he did because he felt badly for me because I was trying so hard.

Some would say I was trying too hard and doing too much. Some would go so far as to say I was blind, because the man obviously had lost interest in the marriage a long time ago. I would say, *"I did what God expects all married couples to do, fight for their marriage."* I was losing the fight for my marriage, but it was still my responsibility to do what I could to keep it. When you are in a fight and you know you are going to lose, you do not throw up your hands and allow yourself to be pulverized, you fight.

I was determined to fight, but I was losing! I was mad at Del ("Help me fight for us!"), I was mad at satan ("Get out of our marriage"), and yes, I was mad at God ("Help us!"). I was fighting trying to hold out long enough to get us to the top of that mountain that all married couples have to climb. I was climbing the mountain for the both of us, while also now carrying his unpacked baggage, but I continued climbing. **WISDOM CRIES OUT**: *Taking on someone else's baggage does not solve the issue.*

I thought if I could get us to the mountaintop, Del would see the other side of the mountain. He would experience that which only couples who hang in there are privileged to experience – the second honeymoon, the one that ends only when death separates you.

I wanted that more than anything else in the world, so for five years I fought the battle. I did not always understand it. I was not always in the best mental (or physical) condition for the fight; consequently, I did not always make the best decisions. I probably even did a lot of stupid stuff. Yet, I continued to fight - failure was not an option. I could not stop fighting until God said stop.

Well, late one evening a month or so before Del left, I was on my way up stairs to bed and God spoke, *"Enough, leave it alone, leave him alone."* I knew it was God. First, I know my Father's voice, second, I did not want it to be Him (I was not ready to stop trying). Thirdly, God had stopped me in my tracks once before. Both times, I was doing something that was becoming baggage, shopping and now shouldering someone else's baggage.

It was time to stop, God was taking the fight out of my hands, it was already out of my control and had been for a very long time. My conversation, if any, was not to be about the state of our marriage or him leaving, just leave it alone. Although disappointed, I must admit, I felt a certain degree of relief. I had done all that God required of me: I swallowed my pride, I humbled myself, I put my feelings on the back burner, I deflected insults, and I continued to love Del. Bottom line, I sucked up the pain (the best way I knew how - shopping), I stayed committed to honoring the marriage vows I made to God.

⊙ഋ⊝ട⊙

I did not realize how tired I was until God released me. Rest had never entered my mind, but with God's release, came rest. I went all out for five years, and the last three, was nothing but pure determination. Let me tell you, there were days when I had to go to the store, I would park and would literally be too emotionally tired to get out of my car. I would sit there until I could gather the strength to go in to the store. By the time Del started moving, I was physically and mentally exhausted. The second week after he left, my body crashed - every muscle in me ached for sleep. My body was coming out of defensive mode; coming out of being upset most of the time, and faking happiness all of the time.

Although careful to keep them in check, my emotions were a mess from years of high hopes dashed down in hurtful rejection. Hoping *every* single night would be the night Del would want to make up, hoping his arms were aching to hug his wife, hoping that differences (whatever they were) had been laid aside. The first month following Del's departure, I could not get enough sleep. Before I got out of bed in the morning, I would make plans for getting back in bed that night. After work and weekends were spent sleeping. Sleep was never so coveted and never felt so good.

Hope against hope had taken its toll. I can look back on those days and I know only God could have kept me. Even if shopping was my outlet, in His time, God took the crutch away when I could stand to face the truth. I said I would leave my baggage and when put to the test, I never went looking for the old baggage. Here's the thing, I no longer had any baggage to go back to, when I gave it to God, He took it away. Then He did me one better, He would not allow me to take on new baggage.

The fight was over, although I lost my marriage, I gained a new

93

appreciation for myself. Some would say, I came out on the losing end, but not so, I also earned God's approval of my life – that is huge. With much sleep, the tension was leaving my body. I had actually forgotten what it felt like to be at ease in my own home, or to enjoy being there. The air was lighter; the heaviness in the atmosphere was gone. Don't get me wrong, I was still hurting, but when God releases you from a situation, (even if you feel that the outcome was not in your favor), there is no denying a weight is lifted.

The struggle to keep my marriage is over and is now in God's hands. Let me tell you something, if you are currently going through a really tough time in your marriage and you are feeling as low as low can go, I say to you, *"Don't give up, keep climbing the mountain until God says come down, stay in the fight until God says sit down. Pray together, I cannot emphasize this enough and I will say it again, pray and move gently around one another."*

My dear sisters and brothers, we give up on our marriages to easily. Fight for your marriage, do not let satan have your marriage, it is a gift from God. Men, you are the family covering, you are the first line of defense in the spiritual (and the physical) battle in your home. Do not give satan your marriage, your family, or your home; no matter the reason you feel you must leave your home, don't do it, instead, take hold of your wife and resolve to pray.

Listen to me, before you dare leave your home (or let her leave), pray with one another every single day for one month, and I believe that your hearts are going to soften toward one another. I believe that once the hearts start to soften, the two of you will be able to make better decisions about your life together. I believe if you do this, the two of you will rediscover a kindness toward one another that has been buried underneath hurt and anger and fighting, the searing pain of hurtful words and misunderstandings and miscommunications, and disappointments.

Start praying, you might start-off not wanting to hold hands while praying, then don't, but pray anyway. One of you or both of you might not want to pray, but one of you, please pray anyway, even if it is two sentences! The prayers will initially be dry and emotionless, but pray the two dry sentences anyway! If you cannot do it for any other reason, do it for God, do it because you stood before Him and made a vow - your marriage at least deserves that.

Satan will try to give you every reason in the world why you should not pray together. He will remind you of your baggage "Go get your baggage!" Do not listen to what he is shouting in your ear. Do not listen to anyone who says, "Don't pray," or "No one will blame you if you walk away." Do not let anyone tell you what you should be doing in your marriage! "Resist the devil and he will flee" (Jam 4:6). If you don't give your baggage to God, then give it back to its rightful owner, when satan flees, give him back his baggage to take with him.

CHAPTER 12

The First 24 Hours

Thankfully, the day Del moved out I already had a full day planned that would keep me distracted and away from the house for most of the day. It was communion Sunday so church would get out a little later than usual, and after church I had dinner plans. Del didn't tell me when he was moving, but I knew the time was at hand, it was the first of the month and he had stepped up the pace in removing things from the house. There was still some moving to be done, but I was certain he would not be returning to spend another night.

Not that it would have made any difference, Del and I did not see each other that last day. He left the house at daybreak, and I was not far behind him, running to my place of solace. **WISDOM CRIES OUT:** *When you are going through a difficult time, besides hanging on to Jesus for dear life, and having a trusted confidant, there should be a special place where you can go to decompress.*

Shopping may have been my pain suppressant, without a doubt, the marina was my place of refuge that kept my head straight. If given a choice between the marina and shopping, as hard as it would have been I would have had to give up the shopping. When I could not breathe, I ran to the marina. After hours of shopping if the pain was still too much to bear, I ran to the marina. When I was tired of being tired, I ran to the marina. When my mind was swirling, I ran to the marina. I would steal away sometimes as late as eleven and twelve o'clock at night, to the marina. It would be too late to get out of the car or even stop, but just to drive alongside the waterfront would calm me down enough to return home and sleep through the night.

The marina was the place I ran to and literally stayed for hours. I have walked that waterfront, from one end to the other, early mornings and late evenings. I walked sometimes with a song on my lips, sometimes with up lifted hands praising my way through the pain, and too many times with tears streaming down my face.

I simply had to be at the marina. There were days when I would park and sit in my car: Napping, reading, munching on a snack, or eating a full meal. Other times if I was not walking or sitting in the car, I would sit out on one of the benches watching the joggers go by; some laboring and bearly lifting their feet off the ground while others effortlessly glided by. I enjoyed seeing the big smiles on the faces of those who were lucky enough to catch a fish. It was a pleasure to watch young children learning to ride their bikes. Their little faces beaming with pride when they peddled a few yards without the help of mom or dad holding them up. It was bitter sweet to see couples strolling hand in hand, then like right out of a movie scene, they would stop, turn toward one another and exchange a tender kiss.

For five years, the marina was the place I ran to and stayed until I could face returning to the reality of a life gone terribly wrong. This particular Sunday morning I was in dire need of my place of refuge. I don't remember what I threw on, I don't remember getting in my car, nor do I recall driving there. I was on full and about to lose it, I had to get to the place I knew would settle me down, and I had to get there fast. I needed to walk, look out at the bay, and feel the cold air on my face. Most importantly, the marina would regulate my breathing.

It was a cold overcast day, with light drizzling; the weather was perfect for the way I was feeling. The water was choppy and the waves that splashed against the pier were white. It was not a pleasant morning and no reason for anyone to be out, except for the die-hard joggers, as for the others; well, like me, maybe they were going through something. I walked until I could bear the thought of getting back in my car to return home. A home that was no longer a home, and had not been one for a very long time, but at least Del was there.

When I returned home and before getting in the shower, I walked through the house. I went in every room, in the kitchen I could feel Del's presence, as I could when standing in the bedroom that we once shared. He was gone and I wanted to face the reality of it, face the dreaded hurt feelings, the plan was to quickly put them behind me and move on. For now, the first order of business was to get myself ready for church.

I could not have felt any lower, yet the thought of missing church never occurred to me until I begin to get ready. My emotions were on edge and unpredictable. How was I going to make it through the service, how was I going to face anyone? Would I be able to get a sentence out without breaking down? Nevertheless, off to church I went.

I was there in body only; my spirit was at the marina to keep me composed. All I can tell you is that I made it through the service. What happened at church, who preached, what the sermon was about, I can't tell you. It was first Sunday, I assume communion was served, did I participate, I have no idea – it was one big blur.

After church, I spent a couple of hours with my good friend before meeting up with her family for dinner. It was actually a good dinner and turned out to be a very pleasant evening. I started to relax a bit and even engaged in some of the various conversations that went on around the table. However, as the hours ticked away, dread started to close in. I was smiling on the outside, while on the inside my heart was full of doom and gloom. As badly as I wanted to get started on dealing with the breakup of my marriage, I knew the first step was to return to the house of pain.

I started getting anxious. What is it going to feel like to walk into the house knowing the person I shared my life with for twenty years was not going to be there? It was getting late, and my energy was beginning to ebb. The thought of walking into an empty house with nighttime approaching started to weigh on me. And fear moved in.

I was afraid to go home, yet I knew I had to face my fear sooner or later - it might as well be sooner. I graciously excused myself, went to my car, stopped and made a mental note that the sun had not come out all day, fitting for my situation - then I went home.

In the hours I had been away from the house, I knew Del had been there. More boxes were in the garage, and as I walked through the house opening closets things that had been there were now gone. Initially I didn't know how I was feeling until I pulled open a drawer; the only thing left was the first card I had given Del years ago. That raised my blood pressure, and I can tell you exactly how I was feeling, furious. He was being nasty, he deliberately left the card for me to find. Nothing else was in the drawer so how could he have overlooked it. He could have at least shown me some compassion by taking the card and then getting rid of it. Wasn't it bad enough that he left, wasn't it bad enough that he took his own sweet time leaving, wasn't everything just bad enough.

I snatched the card out of the drawer, tore it up and threw it on top of the dresser where I knew he would see it when he returned for more of his things. Then I thought better of it, I retrieved all the torn pieces and threw them in the garbage. Maybe I was over-reacting, I really did not know what to think or how to react to any of the events that were taking place.

I calmed down and started to clean up. It was Sunday evening, a day of rest, but I had to clean Del's presence out of the house. Some of the drawers still had his belongings; obviously, he did not want them, so I pitched what he left. I changed my bedding, new bedspread and a new throw. I put new towels and rugs in the master bathroom. I love shopping for towels and bedding so to have new linen on hand was not unusual. I rearranged my bedroom, moving around a couple pieces of furniture that I could handle.

I was pleased with the outcome, but I had to keep moving, I had to stay busy, I wanted no reminders of Del, especially in my bedroom. I had returned home around six in the evening and did not stop working until after eleven that night. I needed to work off some steam. I needed to work through the disappointment, the hurt, the betrayal, the confusion! Most of all I had to tire myself out so I would be exhausted enough to sleep through the night.

No way could I handle a sleepless night, especially not this night. My mind needed some rest, I was puzzled and was asking myself what had just happened, what did I do to this man? God had answered those questions before Del had left, but it still did not address Del's behavior. The night I had cried out in despair, God gave me the spiritual reasons, but what was Del's reason? Clearly, I was not going to work through all the emotions in one evening like I had initially planned, but I sure did try. I wanted to fast forward through the entire nightmare.

I dusted, I vacuumed, and I cleaned up the bedroom where he had spent the last night. As I cleaned everything I put my hands on, I finally got around to cleaning out Del's desk. The remote control to the TV was on the desk, I took it to put it up… okay, to hide it. I knew he would return the following day while I was at work to continue packing and would probably watch TV. I was hoping it would annoy him when he could not find the remote; furthermore, he would immediately know who moved it. I held on to it for a few minutes before putting it back on the desk. I just was not up to it, the damage was done there was no sense in trying to push his buttons. There was no sense in anything - my life was just not making any sense.

I cleaned, I washed, I scrubbed, and I took down and tore up any pictures of Del that was in the house. I changed and rearranged what I could throughout the house. I put out a couple of vases I had never used, and pulled out some throw rugs I had stored away. When I couldn't' find a single thing left I could change, move, cover, clean, or destroy, I then lit as many scented candles as I could find. I laugh when I think back on it, someone walking in could have gotten the wrong idea about the reason I had so many candles lit. Folks, I had to shift the atmosphere in my house.

When I finally felt exhausted enough and content enough with what I had done to rid Del's presence in the house, I blew out the candles, and collapsed into a sound sleep. I got up the next morning, got dressed, and went to work as if nothing new had happened over the weekend. When asked, "*How was your weekend?*" I flashed that familiar smile and responded, "*Fine, how was yours?*" This has been my response every Monday morning since the day Del left.

CHAPTER 13

Only Jesus

The breakup of my marriage was a big disappointment to a lot of people. Many of them have prayed for us and some have attempted to play cupid and mend the marriage. This book is not to hurt anyone, to embarrass anyone or to sway public opinion in favor of Del or in favor me. It simply is what it is, my story – because the truth is, I am not looking too good myself. Furthermore, in spite of how it all turned out I still believe with all my heart that Del is a good man, but I also believe that satan has pulled the wool over his eyes.

After Del left and to this very day my family, sisters in Christ, and so many others have been a great encouragement to me. On more than a few occasions, they have provided some needed comic relief. No matter how bad a situation was, you can always look back on it and find something in it that made you laugh.

Then there are people's reactions that can totally surprise you. Have you ever noticed when a storm comes in your life there's a certain sweetness that comes with it that lifts your heart to take hold of it. As I embraced the kind support from people I hardly knew, it indeed lifted my heart. Knowing I was going through something these sweet people were compelled, though hesitant, to extend their love and encouragement to me. Then there were the friends I have known for years, been to their homes, to their children's weddings, travelled with them – those who I called friend, have not so much as called. Others, for lack of a better term, have been indifferent about the whole matter. The pendulum swings to both extremes disappointment in some and gratitude for others.

There are those who felt as though I shut them out. I can assure them this was not my intention. I was just too vulnerable, and pretty much in a quandary. I wanted to be acknowledged, but I did not want to be fussed over. I wanted (and needed) a hug, but I did not want to be held too tightly for fear I would melt in their arms. So how do you tell someone that? At any rate, there will come a point when the broken-hearted will have to go it alone and a time when only Jesus will do. That time had come for me, a few months or so after Del left I needed some serious alone time, I was at the point where man could no longer console me.

Life was different – even though I forged on, it was a new world for me. Nothing looked the same, sounded the same or tasted the same. I needed a break from everything, friends, family, and especially church. Del and I were still attending the same church, to see him was like pouring salt into an open wound. How was I ever going to heal when every Sunday I worshipped with the very person who turned my world upside down? I still held out hope that we would reunite, but for now, I could not bring myself to look at him. I still loved him, but I had lost respect for him. There were too many contradictions to sort out and too much input from others. There was a time when the input was a welcome, even solicited, but that time had passed.

I felt as though my equilibrium was off and I was floating through the days. The one person I knew I could always count on to be there for me, left. I was thrust into changing my perspective of life. How should I look at life now? Should I trust anyone again? Who am I now? What does single life mean?

The questions were piling up, like the traffic jam I mentioned in chapter one, and I knew, just like I did then, I needed to hear from God. I had to escape into my private space for a while and I definitely needed to escape from the sermons. Every message pastor preached I thought it was about my marriage. I was reading things into the sermons that were not there. I desperately hoped the sermons were about marriage and that Del was hearing it and the Holy Spirit was convicting him. Was he remorseful? Was he still at the church because it was his way of still seeing me on the sly (probably not)? Each Sunday I asked myself, *"Will this be the Sunday he will break down and approach me?"* Oh Lord, the questions were stealing my praise! To make sure he noticed me, I begin dressing intentional, but why should I care if he looked my way or not. Finally, I had to ask myself, *"What are you really getting out of attending church right now?"* Obviously, my focus was not God.

I was becoming increasingly miserable by the day - I could feel the restlessness and frustration welling up inside. I was watching my life go in a direction I did not want it to go, but I was helpless to change its course. As the weeks and months dragged by, I started to, mentally, drift away from family and friends; my heart was being pulled in another direction. I could hear people talking to me, but I was not processing (or particularly interested in) what they were saying, something else had my attention.

Even though I could not do the church thing any longer, I found myself longing for Jesus. There was no more talking to be done, I was talked out, and cried out. I did not want to talk about Del anymore, I did not want to talk about how I was getting along, I did not want to engage in small talk, and I did not want to have any expectations on Sundays or any other day. I did not want church I wanted Jesus.

Attending church was frustrating; the pastor was not getting to the heart of what I wanted to hear. Furthermore, I could not rationalize why Del was still there. He left our home so why didn't he leave the church also, and give me some closure and a thread of consideration. Sunday's became a repeat of when we lived together when I hoped and prayed that each day would be the day he would want to reconcile. It never happened and I went to bed disappointed 1,800 nights, give or take a couple of months here and there of reconciliation. I am finished with forcing my way on God, and on man, I forced my way on Del five years longer than he wanted to stay.

When God released me from trying to fix my marriage and Del finally left, He released me completely and forgave me totally. Yet, if that were the case, then why did I have to now deal with those same expectations Sunday after Sunday? The deed was done, my heart needed healing instead it was being hammered. My spirit was retreating. I did not desire the company I so desperately needed in the months (even years) before Del left or the first couple of months after his departure. I was now longing for solitude and waiting for Jesus to show up.

My withdrawal was no cause for concern, I was aware of my feelings and I felt sure of what I needed. I was also sure of what I did not need. I did not need any more expectations - they were killing me and certainly did not bring me any nearer to closure. I had to somehow reason out what was happening, come to terms with it, and rid myself of expectations of a miraculous reunion.

No matter how unpleasant it was, Del and I attended the same church and that was that. I could not expect anything from him (not even an apology). I could not expect every sermon to be a message about *Marriage God's Way*, or *Life after Betrayal*, or *Men, Man Up!* Just a few sermon suggestions I wanted the pastor to preach on. I wanted pastor to drill Del, make him sweat! Make him repent!

In misery and frustration, I was becoming a little crazy. That is exactly why I knew it was time for some serious alone time with Jesus. It was time to make it the rest of the way on my own. No matter how much encouragement we might receive from others, at the end of the day we are left to the midnight hour to ride it out alone. Although people are praying for you (which helps immensely), and you might even be receiving good counseling; but it is you alone who must put in the work it will take to get to a place of healing.

From the onset of Del's departure, God gave me a lifeline, He dropped a sure word in my spirit, *"I am going to bless you."* I had no idea what it meant, but if God said it, then He would do it, but I would have to do my part. I had drawn strength and encouragement from family and friends, but to finish, I was on my own and I desperately needed Jesus.

❦

My oldest daughter lived with Del and I, she witnessed Del as he struggled to leave, as she also watched me as I struggled to let go. She observed how God seemed to be dealing with both of us, with my permission, she analyzed the chain of events with a great degree of accuracy, I might say. It was pretty amazing to listen to her and although it came at a time when I was despondent, I do recall saying to myself, *"God always leaves a witness."* Everything she said was not in Del's favor and neither was it in mine – she was simply an objective bystander (who never interfered). I smiled and engaged her for a while then withdrew to wait on Jesus.

I did not want my younger daughter to tell me anything, good, bad or indifferent about Del, she and the grandchildren were still in close contact with him. Which was fine with me, I did not care about them maintaining a relationship. She was only months away from turning six when Del came into our lives and now grown, she and Del did have a special relationship. She and the grandchildren needed him, just as much as he needed them, I would never begrudge that.

As all of this was transpiring, family and friends comforted me in their own way. Everyone was trying to understand what had happened and weighing in as best they could. However, I just wanted to commune with Jesus. As I said earlier, I did not want to hear from friends, family or anyone else anymore. Hey, I didn't even want to hear what the church board had to say about the situation. No disrespect, but I was in a fight for my sanity. I was straining to hear from God; each move I made had to come from Him. I was under the leading of the Holy Spirit only, and was accountable to no man. Let me tell you something there will come a time in every Christian's life when you are in the trenches of a situation and in the grips of despair. You will have to shut the world out and press your way into the presence of God. You must be determined to stay put until you hear from Him.

In Jesus, there is only truth and in truth, there is freedom. **WISDOM CRIES OUT:** *Be open to hear the truth. In hearing the truth, it may not be what you want to hear, but we must take heart and accept it.* I knew Jesus would love on me not question me or accuse me, but He was not going to appease me either! Jesus has the authority to tell me explicitly that I am the problem! Jesus does not have to worry about being looked upon as bias. He does not have to worry about taking one side over the other (thus causing hurt feelings or risk losing a friend or a church member or a dollar in the offering plate). He does not have to do the politically correct thing by taking both sides just to keep the peace. I had heard it all and now I needed to bask in the holiness of Jesus.

Yet, at some point in my waiting and in my solitude, I began to reflect back on the last few years. It would have been very difficult to make it through those dark days before and after Del's departure without the loving support of some very special people whom I am deeply and forever beholden to:

- The fervent prayers of my pastor and his beautiful wife, sent to uphold me, via the Holy Spirit.
- My dear sister who didn't say anything, but always sent the perfect cards that said it all, which gave me encouragement.
- My best bud, who spoke so simply to my pain, "I know you're hurting" - those four words fell gently on my heart.
- My gracious family: No fuss, no questions, no blame, no judgment, but hearts that recognized my pain, and we went on with life.
- Words from both my *been there done that* encouragers: My wonderful niece in MV who instructed me (on what I had failed to do), "*Protect your heart*." And my precious sister in Christ who has gone on to be with the Lord, reassuring me, "*You will breathe again, I promise you*." I cannot tell you how many nights I held on to those words until dawn appeared.
- My daughters and granddaughters: My sweet inspirations, they are my strength and my reason.
- My job – no one on my job knew anything, so it was work as usual. "Thank you Lord, that something in my life remained status quo."

Now, I needed Jesus the Healer, I needed a healing. I cannot recall ever experiencing such deep unrelenting pain and absolute betrayal. With the help of the Holy Spirit I had to recalibrate my emotional thermostat – it was deliberately set between lukewarm and cool. Anything warmer than lukewarm would have been too hot for me to handle. I would have over heated and allowed anger to rule the day. With another broken relationship to endure, anything less than the thermostat set at cool, I would have become the ice queen, never allowing anyone into my heart again.

It was a balancing act, which was sometimes misinterpreted. We have to be so careful to not assume or judge others when we do not know what they are going through or how God is dealing with them.

WISDOM CRIES OUT: *Stop thinking when people are acting funny or different, that it's about you, "it really isn't."*

Certainly last, but not least, I thank my long time friend, Pat. Pat knows me well and I knew I would get a reality check from her. Del had been gone for almost four months before I told her. After talking to her for hours on the phone late Saturday night, the release came. Del was gone and I was going to go on with life because that is what we do, live in the moment. One moment at a time, one day at a time, that is what God gives us. Cry at last, give the future to God and embrace what you have, the moment.

Anyway, in looking back at those who supported me I realized that Jesus had not failed me, but had indeed showed up. Jesus showed up in the person of everyone who encouraged me, cried with me, laughed with me, and prayed for me. He came in the persons that loved on me, hugged me, gave me sweet little gifts to ease my pain, and He came in the sweetness and timidity of those who hardly knew me, but loved on me just the same. Jesus even showed up in a magnificent sunrise; as I drove to work one morning out of nowhere the freeway was flooded in a burst of deep orange sunrays. I was immersed in orange sunlight and I immediately knew it was Jesus, He was reaffirming His promise, *"I will never leave you nor forsake you"* (Heb 13:5b).

My dear readers, in longing for solitude to be with Jesus, it was time to be still to reflect, and to honor God. You see, I needed Jesus all the time and all the time He was there. He was always a step ahead of me; He gave me what I needed in the form of family, friends, and sweet encounters with people I hardly knew. Yet, there came a time when my spirit had to steal away from the crowd and into His presence, to a place of gratitude. Although I am so grateful for them and would have had a difficult time without them, we have to see beyond the people that He sends to comfort us, to see Jesus.

When I begin to shut everyone out, it was not to dismiss them. I did not understand it at the time, why I had this deep longing to steal away with Jesus, but my spirit knew. My heart desired to acknowledge, on a deeper level, God as my Comforter (through the people that he sent).

WISDOM CRIES OUT: *When in a storm God gives us what we need, and in return, it should compel us to enter into His holiness and commune* with the Giver. We can so easily become satisfied with and expect the support of people to keep us encouraged. But, no matter how well intended it is, no matter how godly and loving it may be, we must always seek after the One who tugs at our spirit. It is usually to bring to our remembrance that He is a faithful God - who graciously and unassumingly works behind the curtain fulfilling needs. We must be mindful to always look behind the curtain and give thanks to the Giver.

CHAPTER 14

Reasonable Action

In all things, take reasonable action, that is all God expects from any of us. Reasonable action is doing all that is godly reasonable, responsible, respectful, and lawful to accomplish something. When you have done all you can do, short of forcing a square peg into a round hole, it's time to leave it alone and "... *stand firm and you will see the deliverance the Lord will bring you today*" (Exod 14:13).

However, the thing of it is, we are not wired to stand still. We have become quite adept at figuring out how to place a square peg into a round hole. Often times we cross the line of reasonable action and force things to happen to get the outcome we feel entitled to. When we bear our will down on a situation, unbeknown to us we stir up warfare in the heavenly realms because for every human action there is a spiritual reaction.

Spiritual warfare is already a part of our existence simply because God wants to save us, and satan wants to destroy us. All too often, we stir the pot because we think we know better than God, what is best for us. Wrong desires distort good reasoning. When we are driven by a desire that does not line up with the will of God, we are opening the door, grabbing satan by the collar, and dragging him in.

We justify (and sometimes cannot not see) our wrong actions when we become obsessed with what we want. We allow sin into our lives, but never are we equipped to deal with the consequences. However, if we would walk by faith and not by sight, we would train our spiritual senses to seek out the things of God. As we live our lives as children of the light, we learn that an isolated act of disobedience, done in the dark, can have a rippling effect that will never leave our household.

Instead of backing up and taking responsibility for his sin with Bathsheba, David took a deeper dive into sin by trying to cover up his initial sin, sound familiar. God cautioned me, but instead of backing up, I took a deeper dive into sin, thinking it would correct the initial sin. **WISDOM CRIES OUT:** *The closest we can come to correcting sin, is repentance.*

If we rewind the tape when Del and I were reunited, it was initially by phone, he told me then he and his wife were still living in the same house. At that very moment, any reasonable action I had, hit a dead end. If Del and I were going to be together, it was going to be within the context of God's divine work.

Actually, Reggie told me before he made the call that Del was married, but separated. The call should never been made - I foolishly invited sin in. At the time, I had no idea what I was doing; I was blinded by one thing, my desire. Nothing else mattered, and the thing of it is, I was in the church! Furthermore, when God started convicting me, I had no idea I would not be able to appease Him once I married Del! Your desires need to ask the question, *"For what shall it profit a man, if he shall gain the whole world, and lose his own soul? (Mark 8:36).*

I will say it again, God loves marriages, and Del was still married. Let me send you a strong admonishment. You are WRONG when you interfere, hamper, impede, handicap, hinder, obstruct, mess up, break up, shake up, or tear up ANYONE'S marriage, for ANY reason. STAY OUT of other people's marriages, whether the marriage is good, bad, ugly, or turning to ashes – stay out of it, it is NONE OF YOUR BUSINESS.

God has placed a seal around marriages, when someone breaks that seal, *woe to them.* The seal means if the third party in the marriage is not God, then it had better not be you. This is about working out your own salvation. Stay in your own lane, it circumvents a lot of heartache we bring on ourselves and on others. Not to mention a whole lot of regrets and guilt that some of us live with for a lifetime.

We live in an instant gratification culture, and if we can go through the back door to get what we want, we will do it. Dear Sarai, reasonable action is not giving your handmaiden to your husband to bear you a child. God does not require us to commit immoral acts to help Him accomplish His holy purposes.

Ill-gotten gain does not help, but delays and muddies God's plans (but never changes them). I say all this to say, I am guilty, like Sarai (and so many others), I complicated my blessings (whether the blessing included Del or not – I may never know). I compromised myself, Del, and my blessings because I could not wait on God. I wanted Del and I was going to have him, and guess what, God stepped aside and allowed me to have it my way.

Sometimes reasonable action is not doing all that is morally possible. Sometimes it's doing nothing at all. When we do nothing (pray of course), we can then be sure if God moves on our behalf it is His good and perfect will. If He does not move, it is still His good and perfect will, and it is still on our behalf. Our hearts must learn to say, *"The will of the Lord be done"* (Acts 21:14), and then my sisters and brothers, go on with life. We want God to have mercy on us, but we have not learned to have mercy on ourselves. We are too often our worse enemy – not satan, he just gets the credit.

CHAPTER 15

Marriage

How many couples have actually held a written
copy of the marriage vows in their hands?
How many sit down, with vows in hand, and discuss their
understanding of those promises BEFORE their wedding day?
How many have the vows framed and displayed in their homes?
Before harsh words are spoken or adultery committed,
how many couples cling to their vows instead?

Marriage was made to be good. Marriage was made to last. Marriage was made to fulfill humanity's most basic need, intimate companionship; and God's divine purpose, procreation. Marriage was made to glorify God; it is His institute, created to reflect the relationship of the Trinity. Marriage is a beautiful image of Christ and the church, allow me to take that image to another level. Just as the Trinity is a harmonious relationship of order and equality, the perfect oneness of three. Marriage is meant to be a harmonious relationship of order and equality, the perfect oneness of three - husband, wife, and God and out of this sacred union the family is born.

Family is the nucleus of any culture, and every marriage that fails is a thread torn in the fabric that weaves us together as a morally strong society. Sadly, moral decay is destroying the backbone of our nation because we thought it not to our benefit to hold on to what marriage was intended to be, a covenant between husband and wife, but more importantly, a covenant with God.

The marriage covenant has significantly depreciated. We live in a world that is more interested in lobbying for the right to "do their own thing," rather than honoring the vows they made to God. Divorce is no longer a private affair, but big news. The divorce of Brad Pitt and Angelina Joloie has been on newsstands and television stations around the world! The public cannot get enough of hearing about celebrity breakups, and the media cannot crank the stories out fast enough.

There was a time when divorce was an uncomfortable situation to be in and the courts did not make it easy to obtain; consequently, couples were more inclined to work a little harder at ironing out their differences.

We have charted a dangerous course for ourselves and for generations to come with our "live and let live" and "you do you and I'll do me" attitudes. God cherishes marriage, yet we treat it with casual disregard (at best) and flagrant contempt (at worse). We have come full circle, right back to the mentality of the people in the book of Judges where *"every man did what was right in their own eyes" (Jdg 21:25)*. That which God meant to bring honor to man and woman, and glory to His name, society has brought dishonor, dishonesty, distrust, and disdain to.

When marriage becomes too much work and effort or it does not meet *our* expectations, divorce has become the logical answer. In reality, divorce is highly illogical, especially between Christians. Yes, marriage is hard work, but we have been entrusted with the high honor and responsibility, in holy matrimony, to reflect the Trinity. Is that so far-fetched? After all, we were made in *Their* image. *"Let us make man in our image, in our likeness..."* (Gen 1:26).

With God's blueprints in hand, we have the opportunity to build an institute more powerful, more beautiful, more gratifying, and has better fringe benefits than any other institute in the world. God has provided all the materials we need to build a successful marriage: Love, kindness, humility, patience, prayers, and sacrifice.

Marriage is character building; nothing else will ever challenge you to be fair when something unfair has been done to you as marriage will. Nothing else will challenge you to give up your right to be right like marriage will. Nothing else will bring you face to face with the ugliness that so subtly resides in you like marriage will. Nothing else can purge you of selfishness like marriage can. Nothing else will ever bring out the very best in you like a godly marriage has the power of **accomplishing.** However, the question is, can the marriage survive the process?

To get to the best, we have to go through the worse. Marriage can survive if you can remember the part of the marriage vow that says *for worse.* Watch this, "for better or worse" – two extremes at opposite ends of the spectrum. You have to understand what has been done here, a foundation has been laid that captures all possibilities, "for richer, for poor" and "in sickness and in health" – no matter the condition or circumstances. Folks, this is a tough proposition, in life anything can happen to any of us at any time. God challenges us to count the cost before we take the vows.

"Suppose one of you wants to build a tower. Won't you first sit down and estimate the cost to see if you have enough money to complete it? For if you lay the foundation and are not able to finish it, everyone who sees it will ridicule you, saying, this person began to build and wasn't able to finish" (Luke 14:28-30). Your marriage vows, my dear loves, are the marriage's foundation laid by God. Did you count the cost before you started to build on the foundation? The foundation is meant to last, we must build lasting walls on that foundation. Sadly, this is the work that far too many of us cannot finish.

The walls of a city in the Bible were vital; it was a disgrace to the people and to God when the walls were in ruin. Nehemiah wept *(Neh 1:4)* when he found out the walls of his beloved Jerusalem lie in ruin. He made it a point to go there and oversee the rebuilding of the city walls *(Neh 2:11-19).*

God gives us a foundation, but it is up to us to build the walls. As they rebuilt the city walls, the people of Jerusalem had to watch for the enemy. They had to be prepared to fight and build the walls at the same time *(Neh 4:16-19),* are we expected to do any less? Do you really think you are going to build a marriage in peace? Satan knows his weapons to destroy your marriage are ineffective once you finish building the walls of your marriage (upon God's foundation). Consequently, he does everything he can to stop you while you are in the building process. Your job is to watch for the enemy, as you build, and be prepared to fight, not each other, but the enemy.

Marriage is going to cost you something. Can you finish what you started? If not, do not start because for all intent and purposes, you will have unfinished work. There will indeed be some ridicule; oh, you say you don't care because no one has walked in your shoes. I can say, "*You are wrong.*" Anyone who has been married for more than five to ten years, nine out of ten of them have walked in your shoes. They know how hard it is to build a successful marriage, but they will tell you, as I am telling you, "*Don't give up.*"

A couple of paragraphs above, I bolded the word accomplishing, have you ever noticed a couple's reaction when asked how long they have been married. Their entire demeanor changes, and for one magical moment you will catch a twinkle in their eyes that embodies all that God meant marriage to be. They radiate with pride and everything about them suddenly exudes confidence and *accomplishment*. I do believe, this is the one time God allows us to be a *little* puffed up.

When there is, what appears to be, insurmountable problems in the marriage, some people stay for the children's sake and some stay for financial reasons. For heaven sake, do not scorn the reason you are staying or use it as another source of argument. Rather, look at it as an opportunity presented to you to sort out your differences. The reason is not by chance, but divine intervention put in place before you got to the point of wanting to call it quits. **WISDOM CRIES OUT:** *We must always remember that God is at work in everything – He is at the beginning (before you get there), He is at the middle (before you get there), and at the end (before you get there)!*

Throw your hands up toward heaven and laugh, say to God, "*It was fixed from the beginning (before I got there)!*" However, know that it is fixed in your favor! if ! you will humble yourself. Choosing love will indeed keep you humble in your marriage. "*Love does not give up. Love is kind. Love is not jealous. Love does not put itself up as being important. Love has no pride. Love does not do the wrong thing. Love never thinks of itself. Love does not get angry. Love does not remember the suffering that comes from being hurt by someone. Love is not happy with sin. Love is happy with the truth. Love takes everything that comes without giving up. Love believes all things. Love hopes for all things. Love keeps on in all things. Love never comes to an end"* (1ˢᵗ Co 13: 4-8a). If things have gone astray in your marriage, you really can love all the hurt away, love really can usher in a new beginning.

When your marriage is in trouble, look each other straight in the eyes and open your mouths and say, *"We need help, we want this marriage to last, our word is our bond."* Falling out of love is not an option. Growing apart is not an excuse - we should never grow out of our word, but instead, behave like two honorable adults and mature into it.

You do not outgrow a marriage, and you do not fall out of love. Love is for grownups, they understand that love is a choice, which is the best love. It is an extra special love when I decide by my own volition to love you – that is more secure any day than a feeling – feelings come and go. The interesting thing about choosing to love, somewhere in the process, you fall deeply in love.

Marriage can last without one out-growing the other. That is just a pitiful excuse that we have accepted to give ourselves another way out. You out grow fads and trends, not your wife (or husband). We do not have to have everything in common, but we do have to have a common ground, a mutual place reserved only for the two of us. A place that is uniquely ours; where the cares of life are shut out and not welcome to come in, where differences cease, and worldly accomplishments are meaningless. A place where mutuality, commonality and trust are affirmed, and love for one another reign supreme.

Listen, if God says marriage is until death do you part, then please know that your marriage can withstand the test of miscommunication, the test of hurt feelings, the test of disappointments, the test of its not what you thought it would be. If God said until death do you part, then He is more than able to keep your marriage through any storm. God knew your marriage would experience peaks and valleys, sometimes more valleys than peaks, yet He still had enough faith in the union to say nothing should separate you, but death.

You trusted what God meant marriage to be, a vow that should never be broken. God said until death do you part, and your spirit reckoned that to be. Consequently, the ending of a marriage has the potential of being devastating. Divorce was not meant to be a card that would be played. Death is the only honorable conclusion to a marriage, so says God. Yet, the Bible does give one allowable reason for divorce and it is a pathetic one, adultery.

"*Marriage should be honored by all, and the marriage bed kept pure...*" (Heb 13-4a). When the purity of marriage is compromised, God sanctions the dissolution of the marriage. This should give us a glimpse into the profound sanctity of marriage. When we drag our marriage through the mud of adultery, God says leave the unclean act there and walk away. (BUT! If the two of you still want the marriage, He is able to restore it.) Folks, we live in a world where sexual promiscuity is the norm and even glorified.

Sex has been so misused, abused, overused, misunderstood and degraded – that it has lost the honored position God meant for it to have. Sex is a gift to be enjoyed and shared within the boundaries of marriage, and that is, to create godly off springs. I know in the times we are living in that sounds like nonsense, old fashion, and a bitter pill for some to swallow. With that said, let me drop the other shoe on you, by sharing the rest of *Heb 13:4b* "*...for God will judge the adulterer and all the sexually immoral.*"

❦

Remember the Demi Moore/Woody Harrelson movie "Indecent Proposal?" Their marriage could not survive the immoral act they mutually agreed to. Marriage is *holy matrimony*, most couples, when exchanging vows do not hear or comprehend the word *holy*.

Holy is pure, nothing is mixed or added to it – pure is unadulterated, untainted, and wholesome. Marriage means no one else is allowed in; otherwise, it becomes contaminated. When something is contaminated, it loses its usefulness. In "Indecent Proposal" after the married couple agreed to accept character John Gage's million dollar offer to sleep with Diana (the wife), the couple could no longer get along and ended up divorcing. They lost respect for not only each other, but for themselves. The purity they had between the two of them was compromised. I don't know if the writers of this movie realized it or not, but they hit the spiritual nail on the head – the couple lost what their spirits knew was holy. They gave up what money could not buy, nor could it restore what had been lost between them.

⊙❦❧⊙

God hates divorce, but does this mean He does not acknowledge or will not bless a remarriage? Number one, God is a forgiving God; He forgives sin. Number two, God loves marriage and desires to bless all marriages. I believe whole-heartedly that God acknowledges remarriages when forgiveness has been granted, as a result of your repentance for the failure of the first marriage. God is trying to teach men and women how to honor and respect one another, even in divorce. But, as I have talked about earlier, repentance is not always an easy destination to arrive at. But, when truly reached, repentance changes everything. And folks, only God knows the intent of a person's heart.

God does not want sacrifices of sin offerings, *"The multitude of your sacrifices – what are they to me? ... I have more than enough of burnt offerings,..."* (Isa 1:11) - *"Stop bringing meaningless offerings..."* (Isa 1:13). God wants a heart of flesh, a heart that can be broken over sins committed.

⊙❦❧⊙

If you are dating, engaged to, or married to a divorcee, it is important to know if they have sought repentance for the failure of their former marriage. Taking responsibility is good, but I am talking about repentance. Most likely, you will know because they are open about it and can freely admit they are not proud of the failed marriage (no matter whose fault it was).

This is serious business, we are talking about God's holiness and our standing before Him. We have to understand that marriage is a spiritual covenant. When divorce happens we have a moral obligation

121

to respectively and spiritually close the matter, unfortunately we do not do this. This is precisely why so many Christians who remarry have a nagging little secret that they cannot shake – they are not sure if God has approved their marriage.

We must pray for a repentant heart, lest we become complacent, self-justified, and sometimes hardened in our decision to divorce. Repent and allow the Holy Spirit to minister to you. This is so important; your spirit man (woman) yearns for a renewal. We wrongly confuse spiritual yearnings with physical and emotional needs that we want someone else to fulfill. You do not want to get into a situation of vacillating between, "Does God acknowledge my new marriage? Yes no, maybe so." You want to be free of the haunting questions, "In God's eyes am I truly divorced from my first spouse? Or am I an adulterer?"

These are some real questions for a whole lot of *trying to be real* Christians. Your spirit man is seeking the peace of God. The spirit man recognizes man does not own marriage, God does. Even though you are legally divorced in the eyes of the law, you are not at peace. Divorce and remarriage disturbs our spirits with lingering doubts and unanswered questions because Christians know, God hates divorce.

❦

Now don't you "*been married once to the same person*" folks think you are off the hook. Just because you have been married to the same person does not mean you have brought honor to your marriage. It does not mean that God is pleased with the way you have treated your marriage.

Your marriage is in a bad state of affairs; some are on the verge of divorce and some behave like they are divorced. You have cheated in the marriage, only to be taken back. Some have conceived their first child before the I do's were said. Some of you have children by someone other than your spouse. Some of you are just living in the same house for appearances. Seek God's forgiveness because you have not been so right in your marriage. Tell God that you too have been sharing a house with a stranger.

Then there are those who are unequally yoked; one of you is walking with God, the other one is okay with it; however, it is your walk, not theirs. Unequally yoked, even in the best of marriages has its own challenges. One has worldly standards with a variety of views, ideas, and choices, and picks, and pleasures that simply do not align with God. On the other hand, the saved spouse, simply put, is striving to be like Jesus.

When a marriage (whether it is the first or second one, or unequally yoked) is dysfunctional, God desires to restore it to wholeness and holiness. Look, God loves marriages! He wants all marriages to be good! He wants all marriages to glorify Him! I will say it again; man does not know the depths of and sacredness of marriage, God's way.

In Closing

Five or six months after Del had left, I was reflecting over my life when it hit me - three strikes you're out! How could this be happening to me? Before I knew it I was in the clutches of despair. Again, like the night I finally faced the fact that my marriage was over, that familiar feeling of overwhelming anguish came pouring over me.

Again, I cried out to God, the question was no longer what did I do, but, "God, *why me?*" I was blind-sided by the question, did that really come out of my mouth! I had already been well into writing this book and working through a lot of emotions, with a pretty optimistic attitude. It was becoming bearable to look at my future without Del, to make plans without including him was not so painful anymore. I was starting to believe God's promise, which I ended chapter two with, *"For I know the plans I have for you, plans to prosper you and not to harm you, plans to give you hope and a future" (Jer 29:11).* Nevertheless, there I was again, desperately needing an answer.

Folks, the Potter created out of a lump of clay a vessel with a heart that would be pliable in His hands. In spite of the disobedience, the pain, and the shame, God knew I would still have a heart to share through my story what is burdening His heart. God knows I want to have *A Heart Worth Entering Heaven*, that's why me.

God bless you

About the Author

Ms. Cummings has studied, taught, and preached God's word long enough to know it is only His truth that changes lives for the better, eternally. She has spoken at various women conferences and retreats and have had the humble honor of witnessing women being freed from life-long bondages.

Her story is many of our stories, she just had the courage to put it in writing. She knows that she does not walk this journey alone, and as you read, her footsteps will become yours. Read and be renewed, read it again and be blessed, read it again and resolve to live in God's truth.

Ms. Cummings earned her BA in Christian Studies and is an associate minister at her church in California. She is the mother of 2 wonderful daughters and has 3 amazing granddaughters. Ms. Cummings works for a leading healthcare organization, and in her spare time she loves to read, travel, and spend time with family and friends.

Contact Ms. Cummings at JoyCumms@gmail.com
Please note: Joycumms is strictly for praise reports and/or to contact Ms. Cummings for speaking engagements.
This address shall be used to encourage one another and for His glory only.

CPSIA information can be obtained
at www.ICGtesting.com
Printed in the USA
FSHW011946120519
58079FS

9 781973 657606